INSIGHT

ST **PETERSBURG**

GW00337367

Discovery CHANNEL

APA PUBLICATIONS
Part of the Langenscheidt Publishing Group

St Petersburg and Moscow

320 km / 200 miles

BARENTS SEA

NORWAY

Karasjok
Kirkenes
Pechenga
poluostrov Rybachy
Pallastunturi 807
Ivalo
Nikel
Zapolyarny
Teriberka
Muonio
Sodankylä
Severomorsk
Murmansk
mys Kanin Nos
o. Kolguyev
mys Svyatoi Nos
Pomorsky proliv
Olenegorsk
Monchegorsk
Chasnachorr 1191
Kirovsk
Ostrovnoi
poluostrov Kanin
Shoyna
Indiga
Naryan-Mar
Rovaniemi
Kovdor
Alakurtti
Kandalaksha
Kolsky poluostrov
Choshskaya guba
Kemi
Kuusamo
Umba
o. Morzhovets
Nes
Navy Bor
Taivalkoski
Chupa
Kuzomen
Arctic Circle
Oulu
Kestenga
Loukhi
BELOYE MORE (WHITE SEA)
Kamenka
Mezen
Vojnica
Kalevala
Solovetskiye ostrova
o. Anzersky
Ämmänsaari
Paljakka 384
Kostomuksha
Kem
Solovetsky monastyr
Dvinskaya guba
Leshukonskoye
Vozhgora
Kajaani
Yushkozero
Belomorsk
Severodvinsk
Arkhangelsk
Malye Karely
FINLAND
Reboly
Nurmes
Lieksa
Muyezersky
Zapadno-Karelskaya vozvyshennost
Nadvoitsy
Segezha
Onega
Karpogory
Äänekoski
Kuopio
Outokumpu
Porosozero
Medvezhegorsk
Obozersky
Savinsky
Berezник
Blagoyevo
Usogorsk
Jyväskylä
Varkaus
Joensuu
Plesetsk
Mirny
Yemva
Mikkeli
Savonlinna
Suoyarvi
Kondopoga
Pudozh
Shenkursk
Verkhnyaya Toyma
Mikun
Lakhdenpokhya
Sortavala
Petrozavodsk
Nyandoma
Urdoma
Syktyvkar
Lappeenranta
Imatra
Priozersk
Pitkyaranta
Kargopol
Krasnoborsk
Kotlas
Solvychegodsk
Vizinga
Kouvola
Vyborg
Olonets
Ladozhskoye ozero
Vytegra
Konosha
Velsk
Oktyabrsky
Veliky Ustyug
Luza
Kotka
Zelenogorsk
Podporozhe
RUSSIA
Severny Uvaly
Gulf of Finland
Sosnovy Bor
Sankt Peterburg (St Petersburg)
Staraya Ladoga
Vepsskaya vozvyshennost
Belozersk
Kharovsk
Kirillov
Totma
Kichmengsky Gorodok
Oparino
Narva
ESTONIA
Petrokrepast
Tikhvin
Sokol
Nikolsk
Murashi
Slantsy
Chudovo
Kirishi
Pikalevo
Babayevo
Cherepovets
Vologda
Kologriv
Vokhma
Kirov
Gdov
Luga
Malaya Vishera
Gryazovets
Buy
Manturovo
Sharya
Kotelnich
Pechory
Novgorod
Okulovka
Pestovo
Vesegonsk
Poshekhone
Danilov
Galich
Neya
Vetluga
Shakhunya
Pskov
Daa
Borovichi
Udomlya
Rybinsk
Kostroma
Uren
Sovetsk
Ostrov
Staraya Russa
Valday
Bologoye
Bezhetsk
Yaroslavl
Kineshma
Yurevets
Yaransk
Kholm
Vyshny Volochek
Kashin
Rostov
Furmanov
Vichuga
Semenov
Velikie Luki
Valdayskaya vozvyshennost
Ostashkov
Torzhok
Kalyazin
Pereslavl Zalessky
Teykovo
Ivanovo
Yoshkar-Ola
Sebezh
Andreapol
Dubna
Suzdal
Nizhny Novgorod
Cheboksary
Kazan
Nevel
Nelidovo
Rzhev
Moskovsko-vozvyshennost
Tver
Klin
Sergiyev Posad
Kovrov
Dzerzhinsk
Vyazniki
Polatsk
Velizh
Noginsk
Vladimir
Novocheboksarsk
Lyepyel
Demidov
Moskva (Moscow)
Lyubertsy
Gus-Khrustalny
Murom
Arzamas
Sergach
Shumerlya
Buinsk
Vitsyebsk
Safonovo
Vyazma
Obninsk
Podolsk
Sarov
Lukoyanov
Alatyr
BELARUS
Smolensk
Horki
Spas-Demensk
Serpukhov
Kolomna
Kasimov
Krasnoslobodsk
Saransk
Ulyanovsk
Barysaw
Orsha
Smolensko-Moskovskaya vozvyshennost
Kaluga
Ryazan
Mikhaylov
Sasovo
Kovylkino
Inza
Mahilyow
Roslavl
Suvorov
Tula
Novomoskovsk
Ryazhsk
Nizhny Lomov
Penza
Syzran
Krychaw
Lyudinovo
Bolkhov
Spasskoye Lutovinovo
Bogoroditsk
Shatsk
Morshansk
Kamenka
Kuznetsk
Privolzhskaya vozvyshennost
Babruysk
Bryansk
Unecha
Orel
Dankov
Michurinsk
Kirsanov
Petrovsk
Khvalynsk
Homyel
Novozybkov
Trubchevsk
Zheleznogorsk
Yelets
Tambov
Rasskazovo
Serdobsk
Svyetlahorsk
Mazyr
UKRAINE
Livny
Lipetsk

Welcome

This guidebook combines the interests and enthusiasms of two of the world's best-known information providers: Insight Guides, who have set the standard for visual travel guides since 1970, and Discovery Channel, the world's premier source of non-fiction television programming. Since its days as Peter the Great's 'window on the West' St Petersburg has been the most compelling Russian city for travellers. In these pages *Insight Guides'* correspondent in St Petersburg, Anna Benn, has devised a range of itineraries to bring you the best of the city's fabulous tsarist palaces and wealth of literary and musical associations. Three full-day tours combine all the essential sights, while seven further options and three excursions into the Russian countryside cater to visitors with a little more time.

 Anna Benn first went to St Petersburg (then called Leningrad) as a student, when the movements of foreigners were strictly controlled: 'We were all given strict warnings – don't do this, it is forbidden to do that,' Anna recalls. 'In fact there was little we could do except work, and the Russians certainly worked us.' Despite some initial paranoia – she thought the radio in her bedroom was bugged – her first few months in St Petersburg proved fascinating and led to a deep affection for the city and all things Russian. Today's visitors to the city have the luxury of freedom and choice. Anna's advice to first-time visitors today is to take a sense of humour with them, because, she says, 'an element of madness keeps the place afloat'.

This edition of the guide has been updated by **John Varoli**, who also added a new city route, "The City of Lenin", tracing the famous leader's vanishing trail in the city, and an excursion to the Gulf of Finland, a favourite weekend retreat for the citizens of St Petersburg.

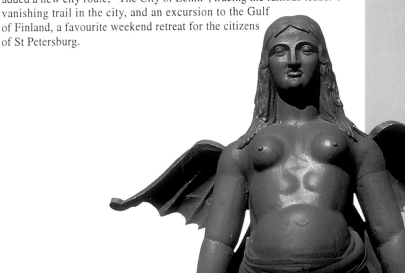

6 contents

10   Moika Boat Trips and Baths catches a taxi-boat and explores the vast network of canals leading off the Moika River. Afterwards it adjourns to a traditional Russian steam bath **51**

EXCURSIONS

Three excursions to destinations within easy reach of St Petersburg.

1   Petrodvoretz – Peter's Palace takes the train (or, in summer, a boat) to the restored palace of Peter the Great, on the Gulf of Finland **57**

2   Oranienbaum is an excursion to a royal palace that escaped German bombing. It offers many splendours, including Catherine the Great's favourite, the Chinese Palace...**59**

3   Gulf of Finland is a trip by train or hire-car to St Petersburg's resort district, which has beaches, lakes and health spas..**60**

LEISURE ACTIVITIES

Advice on what to buy, where to eat and where to visit the ballet or theatre...**65–73**

PRACTICAL INFORMATION

All the background information you are likely to need for your stay in St Petersburg, from tips on transport and telephones to a list of hand-picked hotels **75–91**

MAPS

INDEX AND CREDITS

pages **93–96**

Pages 2/3: snow covering Dvortsovaya ploshchad
Pages 8/9: Church of Our Saviour on Spilled Blood

History & Culture

'To understand our country you have to understand her past' – Mikhail Gorbachev

When you arrive in this city, you may well approach it from the outskirts, passing tall, monotonous, grey buildings from the Soviet era and crowds of people squeezing themselves onto buses or trams. Then suddenly you pass through an invisible barrier and the streets change their character, the buildings are older, the colour scheme changes from grey to pastel shades – pale greens, yellows, pinks, terracottas and golds – and all at once you feel as though you have gone back into the 19th century. There are statues, beautiful railings, canals, and landscapes of perfectly proportioned buildings. At this moment you realise that the outskirts you have left were Leningrad and you have entered St Petersburg.

Peter the Great and Lenin were responsible for the city's two names. And though Lenin moved the capital to Moscow, his presence remained in the streets long after he had gone – huge statues, museums, flags, slogans proclaiming 'all power to the Soviets'.

But where is he now? He's disappeared overnight. You decide you want to go to a Lenin museum, find out a bit more about the Revolution, but it's gone... No, you are told, this building used to house the museum of the October Revolution but before that it was a palace; a well-known prince, Grand Duke, writer or ballerina lived here first. It's now their museum or it's an art gallery.

The traces of Lenin may be disappearing, but the giant founder of the city, Peter the Great, is ever present, sitting on his bronze horse beside the River Neva. The speed with which he created the city has been matched only by the speed of events since his time. Millions have lived and died here and the city rests on the bones of its builders. St Petersburg has seen uprisings and palace coups, revolutions, murders, hunger and wars – one of which reduced it to a shell. But no sooner has it been destroyed, than it patiently rebuilds itself, step by step.

The Tsars

Peter the Great, crowned Tsar in 1682, had a passion for Europe and for the sea. Before he founded St Petersburg he had travelled incognito to Europe and worked in her shipyards. Russia had been, and would continue to be, at war with Sweden for many years, but in 1709 he managed to secure a Swedish

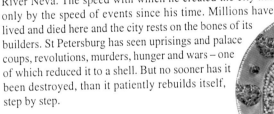

Left: the bronze head of Peter the Great
Right: the Mother of God icon

defeat at Poltava (now in Ukraine). The Peter and Paul Fortress had been built in 1703, but it was only after Poltava that the development of the newly founded city began in earnest. A vital port that controlled the Baltic Sea now lay in Russian hands, and what began as a military base soon turned into a cosmopolitan capital – Sankt Pieter Burkh, which we know as St Petersburg.

Architects were invited from all over Europe and a massive Russian work-force settled in to execute Peter's strict and organised plans, which did not

allow for any architectural idiosyncracies; all roads were to be straight. The city was to be Russia's window onto Europe. Although the land on which it was built had been sparsely populated it was not an obvious base on which to build a city, consisting of lowland, thick forest and swamp, as well as having a harsh climate. Peter was not deterred, and the city of wood and stone rose up almost overnight. The intended centre was Vasilievsky Island but in time the town centre moved, almost jumped, to the opposite bank.

In 1712, the court moved from Moscow to the new capital and after Peter's death, in 1725, the city was somewhat neglected. But in years to come, his daughter, the Empress Elizabeth, and his 'spiritual daughter', Catherine the Great (Catherine II), saw to the city's completion, although they did not follow his style.

Both chose their own Western architects, and left their own distinctive imprints. Elizabeth decorated extravagantly, almost coquettishly, with baroque and rococo flourishes, adding colour, chintz, mirrors and gold (the Catherine Palace, named after her mother, Catherine I, at Tsarskoe Selo is a good example of her taste).

Catherine the Great had an enormous influence on the city. Many historians maintain that she was responsible for completing the major imperial city that Peter had envisaged. She bridged the river and covered the embankments with granite, leaving a more serious, imposing trace of classicism; this reached its peak during the reign of Alexander I, when buildings such as the General Staff headquarters in Palace Square and the Alexander column to mark Russia's defeat of Bonaparte were erected.

Though the official religion of the time was Russian Orthodox Christianity, which enjoyed special privileges and rights in society, some of the greatest Orthodox churches, such as St Isaac's Cathedral *(see page 23)*, were built by Catholics from Europe.

Above: Catherine the Great. **Above right:** Gogol reading to a group of friends from his work *The Government Inspector.* **Right:** the Fontanka, early 19th century.

Art and Commerce

Art flourished in the 19th century, and the city produced some of the greatest writers in world literature, such as Dostoevsky, Gogol and Pushkin. The St Petersburg Conservatory was established in 1862, and its greatest composers include Tchaikovsky, Borodin, Mussorgsky and Rimsky-Korsakov. The Russian ballet was born here, too, and the Imperial Ballet School was founded; the school later trained some of the world's most famous 20th-century dancers, such as Pavlova and Nijinsky. Few countries in the world pay such homage to their writers and artists (nor have many places repressed them so severely). The respect accorded to them is reflected in the number of their apartments and houses that have been turned into museums, faithfully restored as shrines to the past.

From the early years of the 19th century, St Petersburg grew into a rich industrial centre, which attracted influential foreign firms such as Siemens-Schuckert, Thornton, Westinghouse and the Singer Sewing Machine Company, as well as establishing its own major companies. The railway network was built during the reign of Tsar Nicholas I (1825–55) by Austrian and North American engineers. The first stretch to be completed was the line to Tsarskoe Selo from what is now Vitebsk Station. Russia's might was not just reflected in the architecture of the city, but in the opulent lifestyle of the Tsars, which alienated them from their people – peasants, workers and intellectuals alike.

Insurrection

Not surprisingly, revolutionary organisations sprang up, starting with the first Decembrist uprising of 1825, followed by the emergence of populism among the intelligentsia, and the violence of the People's Will Party, which finally succeeded in assassinating Tsar Alexander II after several failed attempts. He had tried to liberalise the country by freeing the serfs, moderating the legal system and creating new rural councils – but for some this wasn't enough. Any insurrection was ruthlessly put down and the offenders jailed in the Peter and Paul Fortress, which soon became a symbol of Tsarist oppression.

Both Alexander III and Nicholas II tried to hold the autocratic regime together as insurrection mounted. Industrialisation brought about cramped and unhealthy living conditions, the cause of massive discontent among an expanding workforce. Russia suffered a disastrous defeat in Japan during the Russo–Japanese War of 1904–5. The general ill-feeling erupted in a series of revolts that Lenin later regarded as a 'dress rehearsal' for the October 1917 Revolution. A peaceful protest led by a priest, Father Gapon, whose message was one of hope, was crushed outside the Winter Palace and the event became known as 'Bloody Sunday'.

After the first revolution of 1905, a parliament, or *duma,* was set up, but the Tsar abolished it a few years later. In the wave of anti-German sentiment provoked by World War I, the German-sounding St Petersburg was renamed Petrograd.

The Romanov dynasty came to an abrupt end in February 1917, when, after a series of massive strikes and demonstrations across the country, Tsar Nicholas II was forced to abdicate.

history/culture

The Cradle of the Revolution

Lenin arrived in April 1917 at Finland Station, where he addressed his supporters from the top of an armoured car. On the night of 25 October the Bolshevik Party seized power, entering the Winter Palace and capturing the Provisional Government. The battleship *Aurora* fired the empty shell that heralded the Revolution. Promising peace, land to the peasants and power to the workers, Lenin formed the communist state of the USSR.

Three years of civil war followed the Revolution. In 1918 Lenin moved the capital to Moscow. When he died in 1924, Petrograd was renamed Leningrad. Starvation, decay, terror and squalid living conditions typified the years until the beginning of World War II.

Despite Lenin's reservations about his leadership abilities, Stalin took control after the revolutionary's death and Russian life during the early 1930s entailed repression and terror. Even 20 years after the revolution, the economy had barely reached Tsarist-era levels, and people lived in terrible poverty. Yet they were sustained by an illusory faith in a brighter future. Fearing Leningrad as a powerful political rival, Stalin had the city's local communist leader, Sergei Kirov, assassinated (the ballet was renamed after his death in 1935), and the purges began. Then, after the German invasion in 1941, came the 900-day siege of the city during the Great Patriotic War. Leningrad lost thousands of people through air raids and shelling, but many more through starvation.

The outstanding poets living and working in St Petersburg before and after the Revolution were Alexander Blok, whose famous poem *The Twelve,* powerfully brings to life the days of Revolution, and Anna Akhmatova, who wrote at the height of Stalinist terror. Most of the houses in which they lived are now open to the public. The musician Dmitry Shostakovich composed his Seventh Symphony during the war-time blockade and it was first performed in the Philharmonic Hall that now bears his name.

St Petersburg Today

After Stalin's death in 1953, the Stalinist system was discredited under Nikita Khruschev, first secretary of the Communist Party and prime minister from 1958–64. The late 1950s brought foreign visitors to the city for the first time in many years. Today, St Petersburg's governor, Valentina Matvienko, places a high priority on the promotion of tourism. Many hotels are being built and in the wake of the city's 300th anniversary in 2003, St Petersburg is one of the more popular destinations in Europe.

To the foreigner, it appears that the city is, as in the time of Peter the Great, looking to the culture of the West. Western firms and joint ventures are cropping up everywhere and the word 'businessman' has entered the Russian vocabulary untranslated. It is becoming harder to distinguish a Westerner from a foreigner in the street. The crime rate, the mafia and

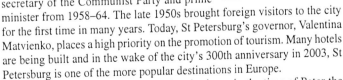

Above left: Nicholas II, the last tsar. **Left:** the 1917 October Revolution
Above: Lenin calls for revolution

prostitution have increased dramatically and people complain of lowering standards, of litter, decay and pollution. What has happened to literature, people ask... how can our young be educated when all they can buy are crime and sex books? Nevertheless, St Petersburg has its own lively art and music scene, which had its beginnings in the underground culture of the communist era.

St Petersburg today is a strange social mix – there is continuing hardship for certain segments of the population, usually those over the age of 45, and especially the retired, but young people have a world of opportunities and are enjoying the city's greatest economic boom since the early 20th century. More and more people are opening their own companies, or working for major Russian and foreign corporations. Take a look on the streets and see the traffic jams paralysing the city, and notice how many of those vehicles are foreign luxury cars. Certainly this is a city on the move. And thanks to the city's popular native son, President Vladimir Putin, more and more investment is flowing to the banks of the Neva, further boosting development and opportunity.

Even so, housing conditions are cramped in St Petersburg, where it is not uncommon to share a flat with several other families. It is a different story outside the town, where many people have *dachas*, small wooden huts, and the transition between life in the city and the country is startling. The Russians make great use of natural resources. In June and July there is a frenzy of jam-making facilitated by an abundance of different berries. While in September everyone rushes out to the fields to pick mushrooms.

Despite the hardships, life goes on. It is still an inspiring and fascinating city to visit. One of the most pleasurable things about tourism today is that you can wander freely around the city and speak openly on subjects that were strictly taboo in the past, and the Russians you always believed to be stern make every effort to debunk this myth: pleased at the levels of tourism, they've made a business out of helping guests explore their fascinating city.

HISTORY HIGHLIGHTS

9th century Creation of first Russian state, centred on city of Kiev. The borders of the northern lands, 'Upper Rus', where St Petersburg was later to be founded, were fought over for seven centuries by Russians and Swedes.

1240 Major battle on the River Neva. Alexander of Novgorod defeats Swedes; becomes Alexander Nevsky.

1672 Birth of Peter (I) the Great.

1682 Peter crowned Tsar of Russia.

1700–21 War with Sweden.

1703 Peter and Paul Fortress completed. St Petersburg founded.

1709 Peter defeats Swedes at the Battle of Poltava. Development of the city begins in earnest. Over 100,000 soldiers and peasants are recruited to start work. City is named Sankt Pieter Burk – Saint Peter's city. The building of Petrodvoretz, the Twelve Colleges and the Menshikov Palace gets under way.

1712 Court moves north from Moscow to the new capital, St Petersburg. Russia becomes a major European power.

1721 Swedes defeated. Russia becomes an Empire with Peter as Emperor.

1725–62 Peter's death is followed by reign of his wife Catherine I, and Peter II. Both prefer Moscow. Anna Ivanovna takes up residence in St Petersburg which, during her reign and that of her successor, Elizabeth, grows rapidly. Winter Palace, Smolny Cathedral and Catherine Palace completed under the architect Rastrelli.

1762–96 Reign of Tsarina Catherine the Great. Hermitage founded.

1796–1801 Paul I. Pavlovsk built.

1801–25 Alexander I's reign dominated by the Napoleonic War. Building of Smolny Institute, the Mikhail Palace, the General Staff buildings.

1825–55 Nicholas I. 1825: Decembrist uprising crushed. Railway between Moscow and St Petersburg built. Russian defeat in Crimean War. Completion of St Isaac's Cathedral.

1855–81 Alexander II. Great reforms and abolition of serfdom. Emergence of People's Will Party, responsible for assassination of Tsar.

1881–94 Alexander III.

1894–1917 Nicholas II. Emergence of populists, Marxists and liberals. St Petersburg becomes an industrial city.

1914–24 The city is renamed Petrograd. Demonstrations and mutinies. Provisional and Soviet Government formed. Abdication of Tsar.

1917 October Revolution; Lenin seizes power; three-year civil war follows.

1918 Capital moves to Moscow.

1924 Lenin's death. Petrograd renamed Leningrad.

1941 German invasion. In September the 900-day siege of the city begins. Death toll of over 650,000.

1945 Reconstruction begins.

1953 Stalin dies. Principle of 'peaceful coexistence'.

1958–64 Nikita Khruschev's policy of de-Stalinisation.

1985–91 Mikhail Gorbachev liberalises the Soviet state.

1991 City renamed St Petersburg.

1992 Boris Yeltsin becomes president.

1993 First free parliamentary elections.

1994 Invasion of Chechnya.

1996 Withdrawal of Russian troops from Chechnya.

1998 Nicholas II and his family finally interred in St Petersburg. Yeltsin sacks government.

1999 Vladimir Putin becomes prime minister.

2000 Putin is elected president.

2003 Putin entertains 40 heads of state in Konstantin Palace during the city's 300th anniversary celebrations.

2004 Controversy surrounds Putin's attack on Russian oil oligarchs.

Left: the face of St Petersburg today

history/culture

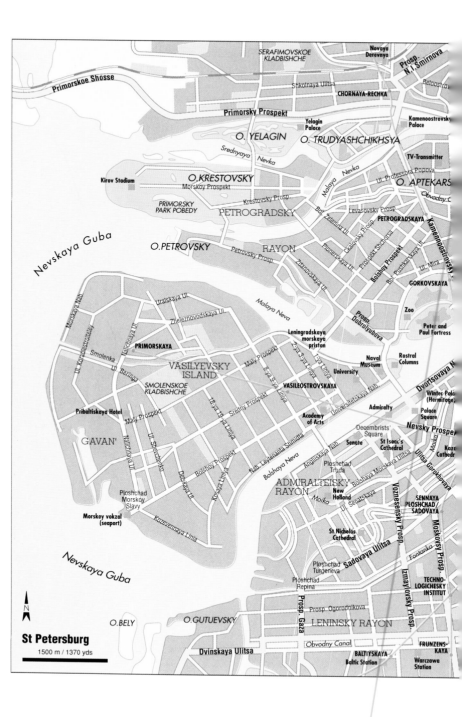

St Petersburg

1500 m / 1370 yds

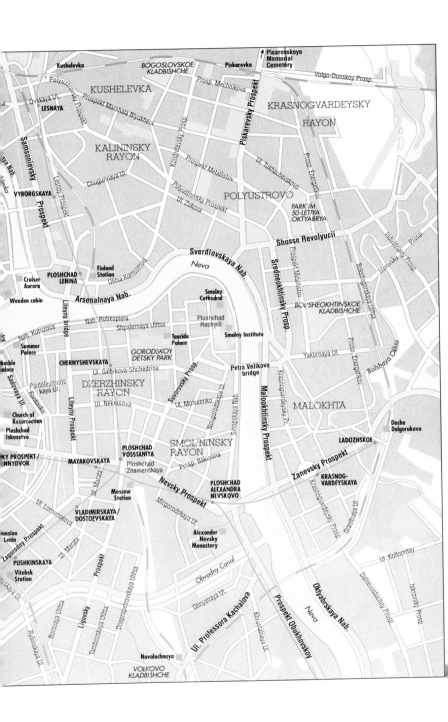

Orientation

If you had only three days in St Petersburg, where would you go? The three one-day itineraries proposed here try to answer this question by combining the most obvious sights with the slightly more off-beat. These tours are best done on foot, although you will probably need to get to your starting point by some means of transport. It is worth mastering the metro system *(see map on page 92)* although I would recommend a taxi until you get to know the town better. Since there are few official taxis, don't be surprised if a private car stops to pick you up. It's the norm here, and cheaper than conventional taxis, but not really recommended for visitors.

Don't be daunted when you hear that the city stands on 101 islands. In reality, you will only be aware of the main three – the first can be called 'the mainland', the second Vasilievsky and the third Petrograd. Once you have taken a trip to the top of St Isaac's Cathedral you will have a pretty good idea of the layout. The main street, Nevsky Prospekt, begins at the Admiralty, the former administrative area which comprises the Winter Palace (Hermitage) and Palace Square. The Nevsky is intersected by three major waterways serviced by boat transport. Day trips one and two keep you almost always in sight of the Admiralty spire.

As the palaces are such a spectacular and integral part of a visit to St Petersburg, the third trip takes you half an hour out of the city to one of the finest. The tzarist court moved out here in summer to escape the humid, dusty urban environment, and this tradition continues. While many locals take to their *dacha* (country house) at weekends, others enjoy strolling in the palace gardens, or driving to the beaches north of the city on the Gulf of Finland, to enjoy water sports and the many pleasant outdoor cafés.

Since St Petersburg is now one of Europe's most popular destinations, expect heavy crowds at major museums during the summer. There is an effort to provide item descriptions in English and most places that cater to tourists now have staff who speak some English.

Always check opening times of museums and restaurants. This guide provides the most up-to-date information available, but the city is continually developing and things change often. Every museum closes for one or two days a week and for a day at the end of each month. For the latest listings of events, check the English-language newspaper, the *St Petersburg Times*, or the magazine, *Where*.

Left: Smolny Cathedral
Right: Peter the Great

1. THE MAJOR LANDMARKS *(see map, p23)*

A visit to the Bronze Horseman, the Admiralty, St Isaac's Cathedral, the Moika River, lunch at the rooftop Victoria restaurant at the Taleon Club, and on to the State Hermitage Museum. This itinerary leads through what was once the most fashionable part of the city and still is the major administrative centre. The most spectacular architecture is found here.

Take a taxi to Ploshchad Dekabristov (Decembrists' Square).

The taxi will drop you in the square where stands the most important statue in the city, that of Peter the Great on a rearing horse. It would be impossible to underestimate the historical and literary importance of this statue. It represents a symbol of the conflicting ideas about the town's founder. In Pushkin's famous poem, 'The Bronze Horseman', the figure comes to life

and bears down on a poor clerk, Evgeny. The cost of lives lost in building this city, and the speed with which Peter pushed for its completion, has certainly never been forgotten and for some, the menacing nature of this statue serves as a reminder. It was cast from a model by the French sculptor, Étienne-Maurice Falconet, and completed in 1782. Although it is always described as Falconet's masterpiece, the head of the Tsar was modelled by one of Falconet's pupils, Marie Collot.

The square in which you are now standing – **Decembrists' Square** – was where, in 1825, Nicholas I's troops fired on some 3,000 mutinous soldiers (and spectators), many of whom had been forced into action by revolutionary-minded young officers. To your left as you face the river are the yellow buildings of the Senate and the Synod, built by the Italian architect Carlo Rossi in 1829–32. Most of Rossi's buildings are painted yellow, as are many of the government institutions in the city. Directly in front of you, across the river, is the embankment of Vasilievsky Island, the University Embankment on which stands the yellow Menshikov palace, the red University building, and, further to the right, the green and white Kunstkamera (Anthropological Museum), which you can visit on another day.

The Admiralty

Leave Decembrists' Square, with the Neva behind you, and walk towards the enormous gold dome of St Isaac's Cathedral. Bear left through the Alexander Gardens. The first statue you come to is of the explorer, Przhevalski (who bears an astonishing resemblance to Stalin). Continue until you reach the fountain in front of the **Admiralty** with its statues of the writers Nikolai Gogol and Mikhail Lermontov, the composer Mikhail Glinka and the poet Vasily Zhukovsky. This was one of the first buildings in the city, constructed in 1705, and then replaced in 1806–23 by the neo-classical design of the architect Andreyan Zakharov, who nevertheless incorporated Petrine elements

Above: detail of relief sculptures on the Admiralty
Above Right: St Isaac's Cathedral

of the original structure. It was used as a naval headquarters and as a shipyard. The building's spire is topped by a weather-vane in the form of a ship – the unofficial emblem of St Petersburg. From the Admiralty, the main streets, Nevsky, Gorokhovaya and Vosnesensky Prospekt, stretch out like an open fan.

Now, with the Admiralty behind you, and the Lobanov-Rostovsky Palace with its marble lions to your right, walk up Vosnesensky Prospekt directly in front of you into St Isaac's Square with the cathedral on your right. To buy your ticket you will need to locate the ticket office, the KACCA (pronounced *kassa*) (open Thursday–Tuesday 11am–6pm). It should be signposted outside the cathedral. Remember to ask for an extra ticket for the *colonnady*. This takes you up a 562-step winding, spiral staircase to the dome, where you have an incredible panoramic view of the city. If you don't like heights, there is plenty to see in the cathedral itself.

St Isaac's Cathedral was built by the French architect, Auguste de Montferrand. It took some 40 years to construct at a great cost in lives, and con-

city itineraries

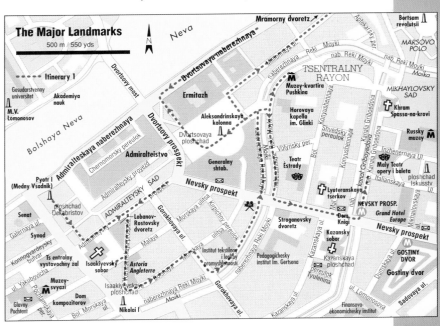

siderable expense. The dome is covered with 100 kg (220 lb) of pure gold and 43 types of stone and marble were used to decorate the interior – you cannot fail to notice the lapis lazuli (blue gemstone) and malachite (bright green mineral) columns of the iconostasis, as well as the many murals. Look out for the statue of Montferrand himself, holding a model of his cathedral, a fitting tribute to the architect to whom Alexander II refused the right of burial in one of the crypts because he was Catholic, not Russian Orthodox.

In the middle of the square is a statue of Nicholas I on a prancing horse, by Pyotr Klodt. Local people have a saying that links this statue with the Bronze Horseman: 'The fool [Nicholas I] runs after the wise man [Peter I], but St Isaac's stands in between.'

Now is a good time for a quick break. Relax in comfort in one of the bars of the **Astoria and Angleterre Hotel**, the terracotta and grey building to your left as you come out of the cathedral. The hotel has two entrances, within a few yards of each other on St Isaac's square. Through the first entrance, you will find a bar and there is another bar through the second.

Turn left out of the Astoria and Angleterre and take the first left up Bolshaya Morskaya Ulitsa, then take the first right up Ulitsa Gorokhovaya. Behind you is the gold spire of the Admiralty. Keep walking (about 300 metres/yds) until you hit the Moika. Turn left and proceed along either of its banks until you come to the main thoroughfare and the green and white palace to your right, which was the home of one of Russia's leading families, the Stroganovs, and the work of Rastrelli, the same Italian architect who was responsible for the Winter Palace. Rastrelli designed many buildings in this city, and they always stand out, with their fanciful, baroque style.

One of the best bargains in town is at **Victoria**, the rooftop restaurant in the Taleon Club. Don't

Above: the Winter Palace
Left: detail St Isaac's Cathedral

be put off by this extravagant-looking club, which you might believe prohibitively expensive. It is true that it's not cheap as a rule, but there's a business lunch available during the week, from noon to 4pm, for only US$8 dollars – and the view is magnificent. Another option is Stroganov Dvor, a nice bistro under a tent in the courtyard of the Stroganov Palace, at the corner of the Moika Canal and Nevsky Prospekt.

The Winter Palace and the Hermitage

After lunch, it's time to see the **Winter Palace,** which houses one of the finest art collections in the world, the **State Hermitage Museum** (Tues–Sat 10.30am–6pm, Sun 10.30am–5pm; tel: 812-110 9625; www.hermitagemuseum.org). To reach the Hermitage, continue walking beside the Moika River until you come to the next bridge (Pevchesky, or Chorister's bridge) and turn left into Palace Square. In the centre of the square stands the **Alexander Column**, which was erected in 1829 and designed by Auguste de Montferrand (architect of St Isaac's) to commemorate the victory of Russian armies in the Napoleonic War, during the reign of Alexander I. This 47-metre (154-ft) column is made from a granite monolith brought from the northern shore of the Gulf of Finland. On the south side of the square is the curved yellow General Staff building, designed by Carlo Rossi. The green and gold building is the Hermitage.

The Hermitage consists of five buildings: the green Winter Palace; the Small Hermitage, built as a retreat for Tsarina Catherine; the Large Hermitage, erected to house Catherine's expanding art collection; the theatre, and lastly the New Hermitage, completed in 1851 after 12 years' work, as the only purpose-built museum in the palace complex. The Winter Palace in existence today is the fourth version. Designed by Bartolomeo Rastrelli, work began in 1754 during Elizabeth's reign. It was the opulent winter residence of the Imperial family until the assassination of Alexander II in 1881. In July 1917, the provisional government based their headquarters at the palace until it was stormed by the Bolsheviks later that year, during the October Revolution.

It would be impossible to visit every part of the Hermitage within a short time, so for now we will limit our tour to a few rooms of Western European art on the second floor.

The main entrance is through the lovely courtyard that you enter from Palace Square. You will be asked to leave your coats and bags in the cloakrooms to the right of the ticket offices. You may also be charged extra to take photographs. The entrance to the museum is to the left of the ticket offices, through the Rastrelli Gallery. You should now make your way to the side of the

Above: Raphael Loggia in the Hermitage

Winter Palace that looks onto Palace Square, to the second floor, displaying many works by French Impressionists, as well as paintings by Picasso and Matisse. If you have time to spare on your way out, there is a fascinating archeological collection of art and artefacts of primitive cultures on the ground floor.

After a visit to the Hermitage, I suggest you try its café. The standard of food and service has improved in recent years.

Boat Trips and Other Options

If you come in summer and don't want to spend all afternoon in the gallery, you can take a **boat trip** from just outside the entrance, which is on the other side of the building, facing the river. These trips usually last for an hour and travel up the Neva River to **Smolny Cathedral**, considered by many to be Rastrelli's other masterpiece.

If the Hermitage is closed I would suggest retracing your steps back across the square to the River Moika, cross the bridge and turn left until you reach the **Pushkin Apartment-Museum** (open 11am–5pm, closed Tuesday and last Friday of the month), at Naberezhnaya Reki Moiki 12. The poet and novelist Alexander Pushkin almost became a participant in the Decembrist Uprising of 1825 *(for more details, see Literary Tour, page 48)*. Audiotape tours are available in various languages, including English. If you're interested in seeing what is on at the St Petersburg State **Capella Hall** (Glinka Academic Choir) in the evening, it's located at Naberezhnaya Moik 20, by the bridge, just off the Palace Square, (tel: 314-1058).

The House of Scholars (turn right out of the Hermitage and walk along the embankment to No. 26) is also known as Vladimirsky Palace, and was built in 1867–72 by Alexander Rezanov for Grand Duke Vladimir Alexandrovich, brother of Tsar Alexander III. He was the one who gave orders to shoot the demonstrators in Palace Square in January 1905.

Otherwise, take a taxi, bus or trolleybus up the busy Nevsky Prospekt and alight at the second intersecting waterway, the Griboedova. Turn left, following the canal towards the splendid, onion-domed **Church of Our Saviour on Spilled Blood** (open Thursday–Tuesday 11am–6pm), also known as the Church of the Resurrection, open to visitors after years of restoration. Tsar Alexander II was mortally wounded on this spot in 1881. Resembling St Basil's Cathedral in Moscow's Red Square, the

Above: taking photos at famous sights is a wedding tradition. **Right:** detail from Cathedral on the Spilled Blood

church took almost 25 years to complete. At No. 14 you will find the **Chaika** (Seagull) bar, open until 3am, where bar meals are available.

The **Marble Palace** (Mramorny Dvoretz) is situated near the Field of Mars (Marsovo Polye), on Ulitsa Millionnaya – Millionaires' Row. In Soviet times, the street was known as Ulitsa Khalturina, after S.N. Khalturin, who planted a bomb inside the Winter Palace in 1880. The old pre-revolutionary street name has been unashamedly reinstated, however, so the city can once again boast a Millionaires' Row.

Walk up Ulitsa Millionnaya from Palace Square; it runs behind the Hermitage Buildings. En route, look out for the Atlantes that support the porch of the New Hermitage building, designed by the 19th-century German architect Leo von Klenze. The walk is about 800 metres/yds, ending just before the Field of Mars. You will see the grey facade of the palace to your left, in a courtyard.

The Marble Palace was designed by Antonio Rinaldi at the behest of Catherine the Great, and intended as a gift for her lover and supporter, Grigory Orlov, who died before it was completed. It was lived in by a Grand Duke before the Revolution, and in 1937 it became a Lenin Museum. Now it is part of the Russian Museum and holds various temporary exhibitions. It may look somewhat austere from the outside, but do look inside, even if you are not going to see an exhibition there – the interior is wonderfully extravagant, with staircases built and decorated with marble and gold.

2. THE TSARS' CITY *(see map, p28)*

A visit to Peter the Great's wooden cabin and the Peter and Paul Fortress, a walk along the shore, then on to the Summer Palace and the Russian Museum. Book Sadkos, Rossi's, Chopsticks or Restaurant Europe for an evening meal.

Take the metro (or taxi) to Metro Station Gorkovskaya.

The **Peter and Paul Fortress** (grounds open daily 10am–10pm) does not open at the crack of dawn, so you have the ideal amount of time to take a leisurely walk from the metro down to the river to see Peter the Great's **Wooden Cabin** (open Wednesday–Monday 10am–5.30pm, closed last Monday of the month and in winter). Exit the metro, bear right, and with Kamenoostrovsky Prospekt in sight to your left, walk through Alexandrovsky Park until you reach the river. Just before the bridge, turn left and walk along the river embankment. When you come to some steps on your right, on which sit stone lions brought from China at the end of the 19th century, the Wooden Cabin is directly to your left, secluded among the trees. Although protected by stone on the outside, inside you will be able to see a perfectly preserved two-roomed hut, made out of rough pine in just three days in 1703.

When you go back to the Fortress, enter through the main, St John's Gate. You are now on **Zayachy** or **Hare Island**. The day the Fortress was completed – 27 May 1703 – is considered to be the day that the town was founded.

Above: Peter's coat of arms

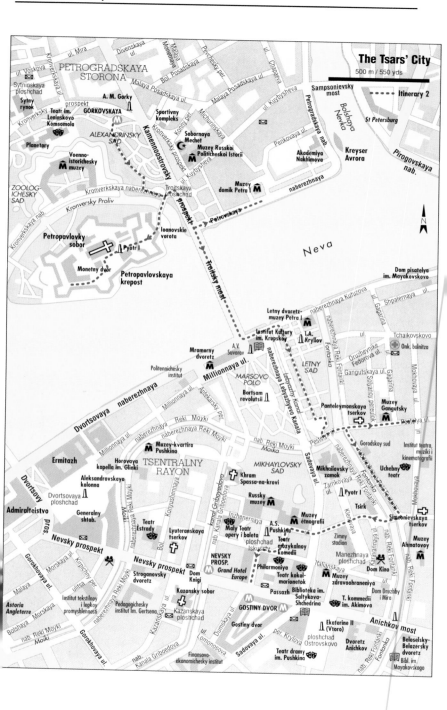

The Tsars' City

500 m / 550 yds

---- Itinerary 2

It was built by Peter the Great to defend the banks of the Neva from the Swedes and served as a fortress until the early 19th century, when it became one of the most deathly prisons of Tsarist Russia. (For detailed information and a timeline on Russian Tsarist history, visit www.russianhistory.org.)

Buy your tickets at the KACCA on the right-hand side. There are various museums (Thur–Tues 11am–6pm, closed last Tues of month) within the Fortress, but your ticket enables you to enter them all. Of particular interest is the **Cathedral of St Peter and St Paul**. To get there, come out of the ticket office and walk straight into the centre of the Fortress through the next gate, St Peter's. The yellow building of the cathedral will be obvious and it is from here that the famous 122-metre/400-ft spire rises. Peter sought a new departure from traditional Russian architecture and commissioned Domenico Trezzini in 1712 to design what became a baroque masterpiece. Inside you will see the tombs of most of the Russian emperors and empresses. Peter the Great died in 1725, eight years before the cathedral was completed, and lies in a white-marble sarcophagus in the far right-hand corner. Monarchists will be proud to see that

Vladimir Kirilovich, who was the nearest surviving relative of Nicholas II and who lived in exile in Paris, was buried here in 1992. In 1998, exactly 80 years after their murder at Ekaterinburg, the last Romanov Tsar, Nicholas, and his family were reburied here, except his son Alexei and one daughter, who some say is Olga, others say Anastasia, which fuels the legend that these children were spared.

Also take a look at the prison cells in the **Trubetskoy Bastion**. To get there, turn left as you come out of the cathedral and follow the path round beside a pale pink building. The entrance is in the yellow building on the corner. Peter the Great's son, Alexis, was murdered here in 1718 after being tortured by his father, who suspected the boy of plotting against him. Dostoevsky served time here, as did Lenin's brother, Alexander.

Above: nave at Peter and Paul cathedral
Right: cathedral spire seen over fortress wall

city itineraries

If you hear an unearthly sound at midday, it is only the Fortress cannon going off. Visitors jump in fright while locals merely check their watches and carry on regardless.

Cross Troitsky Most (bridge), turning left when you reach the opposite embankment, Naberezhnaya Kutuzova. This is a 10-minute walk. If your legs are tired, take a bus one stop over the bridge. The black-and-gold wrought-iron railings to your right lead in to the lovely **Summer Gardens**, filled with marble statues and lime trees. In the northeast corner of the gardens stands Peter's modest **Summer Palace** (Wed–Mon 11am–5pm, closed 11 Nov–end April), tickets for which can be purchased at the tea pavilion. The Palace, one of St Petersburg's first stone edifices, was commissioned by Peter and completed in 1714 by Domenico Trezzini, whose works are typical of early Russian baroque. Peter spent most of his summers in the unheated Palace, overlooking the Fontanka Canal and Gardens. The colder months he spent at the Winter Palace.

You are probably looking forward to lunch by now, so continue through the gardens as far as the pond. Exit after the urn statue, through a gate bordered by double-headed eagles. Opposite you is the terracotta **Mikhailovsky Castle** (Wed–Sun 10am–5pm, Mon till 4pm) where Paul I was assassinated. The building houses some of the exhibits from the Russian Museum, but is still under restoration. A good lunch option is the **Prival.com Café**, in a basement on the corner of the Field of Mars and the Moika Canal. This café was a popular meeting place for artists before the 1917 Revolution. Or you can walk to Sadovaya Ulitsa 11, to **Onegin**, one of the most stylish places in the city, but expensive.

The Russian Museum

After lunch, walk along the Fontanka Canal with Mikhailovsky Castle on your right, until you come to the next bridge. Turn right over the bridge into Inzheneryaya Ulitsa. Pass the **circus** on your right then cross over Sadovaya Ulitsa. Keep walking until you reach Ploshchad Iskusstv (Square of the Arts). **The Russian Museum** (open Wed–Sun 10am–5pm, Mon till 4pm) stands in the middle of the square, to your right as you come in. Don't confuse it with the first museum you pass; this is the Museum of Ethnography *(see below)*.

The yellow classical building of the Russian Museum was built by Rossi from 1819–25 for Grand Duke Mikhail, the younger brother of Alexander I and Nicholas I. Unlike the Hermitage, it houses only Russian items and is a smaller, more manageable museum. The exhibits cover almost 1,000 years of the history of Russian art, including folk art, from an amazing icon collection to works of the present day. Don't miss the icons or the paintings from the second half of the 19th century – particularly those of Ilya Repin, the leading Russian realist painter – as well as the Russian art of the avant garde (Malevich, Filonov). And always watch out for the temporary exhibitions, where you may see some of the finest contemporary art.

If you have time, the **Russian Ethnographical Museum** (open Tues–Sun 10am–5pm, closed last Fri of the month) next door is also well worth a visit, for its dated yet fascinating displays of the everyday life of the peoples of Russia in the 19th and 20th centuries. Children would find this much more amusing than the Russian Museum.

While you are in Ploshchad Iskusstv you may like to take the opportunity to check what is currently being performed at the **Shostakovich Philharmonia** (Mikhailovskaya Ulits, 2), and at the **Mussorgsky Theatre of Opera and Ballet** (Ploshchad Isskusstv 1). In the middle of the square stands a famous statue of Alexander Pushkin by one of the city's leading sculptors, Mikhail Anikuschin.

Cross over the square and, with the Russian Museum directly behind you, walk down Mikhailovskaya Ulitsa. On the right is one of the city's most luxurious hotels, the **Grand Hotel Europe** – Russia's first 5-star hotel. It dates back to the 1820s and combines historic splendour with luxurious modern facilities (for further information about the history, the suites and celebrity guests, log on to www.grand-hotel-europe.com). **Sadkos**, a bar that is part of the hotel, has its own entrance on the right, after the main hotel entrance. You can also just have a drink in the hotel itself. You can either eat at Sadkos, Rossi's or Chopsticks (all situated inside the Grand Hotel Europe) or if you feel extravagant, try the hotel's Restaurant Europe.

Left: Romany children and relaxing in the Summer Garden.
Above: icon from the Russian Museum

3. PALACE RETREATS *(see pull-out map)*

The suburbs of St Petersburg were once home to dozens of palaces belonging to the Romanovs and other powerful families. Today, there are a few worth visiting, though the tourist crowds have yet to arrive.

It is advisable to rent a car or hire a taxi for the day.

The finest and most luxurious palace is the Catherine Palace in Pushkin (also known by its pre-1917 name, Tsarskoe Selo), while Peterhof Palace in Petrodvoretz *(see page 57 for more details)* is more modest, and better known for its fountains and parks. Other magnificent structures include Pavlovsk, Gatchina, Oranienbaum *(see page 59)*, and the Alexander Palace, which is also in Pushkin, not far from the Catherine Palace. In 2003, Russia rebuilt the **Konstantin Palace** in Strelno, on the Peterhof Shosse, the road leading to Peterhof. This magnificent 18th–19th-century building now serves as an official state residence, and it was here that President Putin entertained 40 heads of state during the city's 300th anniversary in May 2003. The exterior is impressive, but its interior is mediocre, as is the park. It is open to the public, but since it's a government residence and subject to high security, it's best to book a visit through a tour agency.

Each palace described here requires nearly a full day, but if you plan things right and get up early you should be able to squeeze in two in a day.

The Tsars' Summer Palace

Catherine Palace (open 10am–7pm daily, closed Tues and last Mon of the month) was the tsars' and tsarinas' official summer residence, where they held court and received foreign emissaries. You can reach it by train from the Vitebsk

Above: facade of the Catherine Palace. **Left:** cupid in the palace
Right: amber panels recreated for Catherine Palace

Railway Station not far from the city centre (return trip costs no more than US$2), but navigating the suburban train system is not easy, and few signs are in English. You can also take the *marshrutny taksi* from Moskovskoye metro station in the south of the city (less than US$1), taking care to get the one that goes to Pushkin, as not all do. But unless you're looking for an adventure, I strongly recommend you hire a car or taxi for the day. This will cost about US$50–60, but the day will be problem-free. Public transport to the suburbs is a major headache, even for Russians.

You will know when you have arrived, on account of the bright turquoise and gold of the palace shining through the trees. Peter the Great's wife, Catherine I, chose the site in around 1718, intending a stone country house as a surprise for her husband who was away for two years in Poland, learning new trades and studying architectural and technological developments. It seems to be the fate of each palace to be altered by successive monarchs and Peter's daughter, the Empress Elizabeth, decided to improve on the country house when she came to the throne in 1741. She asked the architect, Bartolomeo Rastrelli, to design a royal residence modelled on Versailles and named it Catherine Palace in honour of her mother. Although it was added to by subsequent rulers, particularly Catherine the Great, whose architect, Scotsman Charles Cameron, gave it a more stately feel, it is above all Elizabeth's creation. It was not finished in her lifetime, but the extravagant baroque design was symbolic of the mood that predominated during her reign.

The town expanded rapidly in the late 19th and early 20th centuries, and it is said that Tsarskoe Selo was the first city in Europe with electric street lighting. It developed as a popular summer resort – the climate is much better here than in St Petersburg – and after the Revolution many of the houses of the nobility were turned into sanatoria and holiday homes for children. In 1924 it was renamed Detskoye Selo (Children's Village). The name changed again in 1937 to Pushkin, as the poet had studied at the Lycée in 1811, aged 12 (the Lycée, attached to the Palace, has the same public opening times). In 1941, Tsarskoe Selo was occupied by the German army, which left both the city and the Palace in ruins. The Palace has undergone extensive restoration since then.

The ticket offices, KACCA, are in the main part, along the 300-metre (980-ft) facade. You may find several tour groups going round, and if you want to find out the finer details, it is well worth tagging on to one of these. As in many palaces and museums, you will be asked to wear *tapochki* – slippers which you tie on over your shoes to prevent damage to the floors (they also help to polish them). In every room there will be an attendant, usually a *babushka* – which literally means old woman. These formidable ladies can seem very fierce and take any opportunity to tell you off.

Like the exterior, the interior is a mixture of different architectural styles: the baroque of Rastrelli and the classicism of Cameron. The spacious **Great Hall**, with its mirrors, wood carvings and glistening gold is perhaps the most sumptuous of all.

One of the mysteries of the palace is the absence of the amber panels given to Peter the Great by Friedrich-Wilhelm, King of Prussia, which disappeared after the German occupation. Russian officials blamed the occupiers, but historians Adrian Levy and Catherine Scott-Clark suggest in *The Amber Room* that Russians destroyed the rooms. Rumours abound that they have been found, but sadly they *are* only rumours. Still, in May 2003 Russian craftsmen, with a US$3-million donation from Germany's Ruhrgas, completed work on an exact replica of the Amber Room.

There is another, smaller palace in the grounds – **Alexander Palace** (Wed–Mon 10am–4.30pm), presented to Alexander I by his grandmother, Catherine the Great, on the occasion of his marriage. Designed by Giacomo

Quarenghi in 1792, it is less ornate, more classical. This is where the last Romanov family lived under house arrest before they were executed in Ekaterinburg in 1918.

There is a great deal to see in the park and I would recommend that you first walk away from the house, past the **Upper** and **Lower Baths** to the **Hermitage**, then round the great pond, in the direction of the Alexander Park and Palace. Don't miss the Fountain of the Milkmaid with the broken pitcher, inspired by a La Fontaine fable, or the Caprice. Also make sure you see the courtyard side of the palace, with its impressive railings. If you have time, there is **Pushkin's** *dacha* (Wed –Sun) and a carriage museum (Thur–Mon).

Pavlovsk

As **Pavlovsk** (open Sat–Thur 10am–5pm, closed first Mon of the month) is the smallest of the palaces, it is the best one to visit in the afternoon, after an early lunch or in combination with a visit to Tsarskoe Selo. Charles Cameron was the architect chosen to build this palace for Catherine the Great's son, Paul, and his wife, Maria Feodorovna, as well as to redesign the gardens in the then-fashionable English style. Later on the Italian architect, Brenna, was brought in. The land had originally been chosen for the royal hunt because of all the elk and wild fowl. In 1944, the Germans set fire to the Palace and the park was devastated as thousands of trees were cut down. Since then many have been replanted and the restoration work to the building has been completed.

The rooms inside the Pavlovsk – of which the finest are those upstairs – reflect the styles of the various architects: Cameron, Brenna, Quarenghi, Rossi

Above: in the park of Catherine Palace
Right: the Pavlosk State Bedroom and foyer

and Voronikhin. Tsar Paul I's own character comes across in the **Hall of War** as well as the **Throne Room** and the **Hall of the Maltese Knights of St John**. His wife's **Hall of Peace** forms a pleasant contrast. Look out for the tapestries in the Carpet Room, representing motifs from Cervantes' novel *Don Quixote*, as well as for the French furniture, the embroidered French curtains in the **Greek Hall**, and in the Hall of Peace the tripod-vase of crystal and red-gold made in the St Petersburg glass factory in 1811.

The gardens are huge (600 hectares/1,482 acres), so keep to the pavilions nearer the palace, such as the **Temple of Friendship**, marking the friendship between Maria and her mother-in-law; the **Centaur Bridge**, the **Cold Baths**, the **Apollo Colonnade** and the **Pavilion of the Three Graces**.

Gatchina Palace

Construction on **Gatchina Palace** began in 1766, when Catherine the Great commissioned the Italian architect, Antonio Rinaldi, to build a suburban residence for her lover, Count Grigory Orlov. After his death in 1783 Catherine gave the palace to her son, the future Emperor Paul I, who commissioned Vincenzo Brenna to remodel it. Paul's life in Gatchina was a sort of banishment. His mother detested him, and he returned her feelings, blaming her for the death of his father, Peter III. Paul, a difficult character and a fanatical disciplinarian, turned Gatchina into his fiefdom, and drilled his guards' regiments nearly every day.

Despite the imposing classical exterior, Gatchina's interior is of little interest, and the grounds are unkempt. The palace was almost destroyed in World War II, and even today less than half of it has been restored.

4. THE CITY OF LENIN *(see pullout map)*

Visit the Finland Station, the Museum of Russian Political History, the Museum of the Secret Police, the Lenin Museum and other sites that commemorate the 1917 Revolution, the Soviet era and its aftermath.

Take the metro or a taxi to the Finland Station to start the tour.

After decades of Soviet suppression of its tsarist past, St Petersburg can once again bask in its status as the fount of Imperial Russian culture in all its brilliance. Unfortunately, there has been an effort to forget the more unsavoury moments in its history, such as the Bolshevik seizure of power

in November 1917 and the subsequent dictatorship. In Soviet times, hundreds of statues to Bolshevik revolutionaries decorated the city, but today only a few remain. If you arrive by plane, you'll see the most prominent Lenin statue, a glaring, 14-metre (46-ft) high figure, by leading sculptor, Mikhail Anikushin, still standing on Moskovsky Prospekt .

Behind the statue is the city's most prominent example of the Stalinist architectural style – a massive structure built just after World War II to house the non-existent government of the Russian Federated Soviet Socialist Republic (RFSSR), of which Leningrad was destined to be the capital; those plans were shelved after Stalin's death.

Above: Lenin at Finland Station
Left: sailors on board the *Aurora*

city itineraries

Finland Station

The best place to begin a tour of the City of Lenin is **Finland Station**, the exact spot where Lenin arrived in Petrograd from Switzerland, with assistance from German spies, in April 1917. To the left of the station you can see the train on which he arrived. On the square stands one of the world's most famous Lenin statues, depicting him on a military vehicle, exhorting the masses to rise up.

Take a short walk across the Sampsonievsky Bridge to the **Aurora Cruiser** (10.30am–4pm, closed Mon and Fri). Soviet leaflets once told how this ship 'heralded a new era in the history of mankind'. Today, Russians joke that the *Aurora* is the most powerful naval warship ever built. One shot was enough to destroy the largest country on earth, they quip sarcastically. At 9.45pm on 25 October (according to the Julian calendar; 7 November, by the Gregorian calendar) the *Aurora* fired a blank round – a signal for the Bolshevik forces to storm the Winter Palace, the seat of the Provisional Government. Once inside, the Bolsheviks arrested the government ministers who were meeting in the Tsar's Small Dining Room. Today, there is a small plaque in this room commemorating that fateful night in 1917. Though Sergei Eisenstein's 1927 classic film, *October*, depicts hordes of workers, peasants and sailors storming the Winter Palace, in fact, only a handful of revolutionaries were involved and they easily put an end to the disintegrating Provisional Government.

Before you make your way to the Winter Palace, stop off at the **Museum of Russian Political History** (Fri–Wed 10am–6pm; tel: 233-7052) on Ulitsa Kyubisheva 2. This art-nouveau masterpiece was built in 1906 for the prima ballerina, Matilda Kshesinskaya, a former love of Nicholas II before he became tsar.

For a proletarian revolutionary, Lenin had particularly bourgeois tastes and settled in the luxurious **Kshesinskaya Residence** after arriving at the Finland Station. From the balcony, he announced his revolutionary proclamation, now known as the 'April Theses', to hundreds of supporters gathered on the square below. A memorial plaque on the facade commemorates the event. In Soviet times, the Museum of the Revolution was located here.

It is out of chronological order, but as it's nearby, on Kamennostrovsky Prospekt 26/28, you may want to visit the **Museum Flat of Sergei Kirov** (Sat–Sun 11am–6pm, Tues and Fri 11am–5pm; closed last Tues of the month; tel: 346-0217). Kirov, the Leningrad Communist Party Leader, was assassinated in his office in Smolny in 1934 – many believe by Stalin's henchmen – and his death triggered the Great Terror. The museum- flat is interesting not only because it belonged to a famous communist leader, but because it's

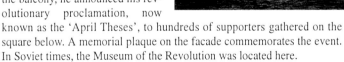

Above: the *Aurora* at anchor

one of the few places in the city that
still has a genuine 1930s interior. It
also shows how well the Soviet elite
lived compared to the millions of
workers, who were crammed into
wretched communal flats.

Make your way down Kamen-
nostrovsky Prospekt but before you
cross the Troitsky Bridge, stop at
the small park on your left. At the
northern end of the park you will
see a large boulder mounted on a
platform. Erected in the mid-1990s,
it is the city's only monument to the
victims of Soviet repression. The
boulder is a piece of rock from the
first Soviet gulag prison, on Solovetsky Island near the Arctic region,
commonly referred to as 'Solovki'.

Around the platform is a phrase from a poem by Anna Akhmatova honour-
ing the millions who died at the hands of the Soviets.

The Field of Mars and Palace Square

The bridge leads you directly to the **Field of Mars**, which was once called
Square of the Victims of the Revolution. That was the name given to it by the
Bolsheviks just after 1917, and revolutionaries who had given their lives
for the cause were buried here in a mass grave. In the mid-1950s, an eternal flame was added. Even today you may see Russian newlyweds, straight
from their wedding, paying homage to the fallen revolutionaries. In one
corner of the Field of Mars is the **Marble Palace**. Since 1993, it's been a part
of the Russian Museum, but before that it was the Central Museum of Lenin.

Next, go down Millionaya Ulitsa to **Palace Square**. This regal and tranquil square is perhaps the most beautiful place in the city. But 100 years

ago, in January 1905, it was the
scene of Bloody Sunday, a massacre
of hundreds of peaceful protestors
that triggered the First Russian Revolution, eventually crushed by a
ruthless tsarist system.

Palace Square has also had a recent
revolutionary history. Here in August
1991 tens of thousands came out to
demonstrate in support of former
Russian president, Boris Yeltsin,
when he held out in Moscow against
coup plotters hoping to restore a hard-
line Soviet regime. But on many
occasions during the 1990s, the

Top: Political History Museum
Above: facade of the General Staff Building. **Right:** Smolny Cathedral

square also served as the rallying point for tens of thousands of communist supporters protesting against Yeltsin's reforms. Today, the square is often used for celebrating festive national holidays and special events.

Walk across the square and then across Nevsky Prospekt to the corner of Gorokhovaya Ulitsa 2. This building now houses the **Museum of the History of the Secret Police** (Mon–Fri 10am–6pm; tel: 312-2742). In this building, in 1918, Felix Dzerzhinsky founded the first Soviet secret police force, the Cheka, predecessor of the KGB. But its police pedigree goes back further: the tsarist-era Police Administration was also based here. The museum has a great collection of reports from secret agents, letters from political prisoners and photos of government informants.

For a look at the current secret police, you might want to pass by Liteiny Prospekt 4, the headquarters of the Federal Security Services (FSB), the successor to the KGB, which still strikes fear into the hearts of Russians today. This building served as KGB headquarters in Soviet times and has been nicknamed the Big House ever since it was built in 1937. If you want to take a photograph, do it quickly and discreetly, or the police might detain you.

Go about 2 km (1 mile) to the end of Shpalernaya Ulitsa and you'll see **Smolny Cathedral** and the **Smolny Institute for Well-born Young Ladies**, where, on 26 October (8 November in the Gregorian calendar) Lenin proclaimed the creation of the Soviet Socialist Republic. Smolny became Bolshevik headquarters in September 1917 after the Bolsheviks had been kicked out of the Kshesinskaya residence by the Provisional Government in July and forced to go underground, until the Kornilov Affair in September paved the way for their legal return.

Smolny is now the seat of the city governor, and is a highly secure government building. Admittance to the small **Lenin Museum** (Mon–Fri 10am–5pm, Sat 11am–3pm; tel: 278-1461) can only be arranged by calling at least a day in advance. A visit is highly recommended. On display are rare socialist-realist portraits of Lenin, Stalin and others associated with the Revolution, plus photos, documents and other items.

city itineraries

5. THE ALEXANDER NEVSKY LAVRA *(see map, p41)*

Smolny Cathedral and the Alexander Nevsky Monastery, built in the time of Peter the Great.

Take a taxi to Smolny or metro to Chernyshevskaya followed by bus No 26 to Ploshchad Rastrelli. If you leave out Smolny, go by metro to Ploshchad Alexander Nevskovo.

If you do not want to get up at the crack of dawn, limit your trip to the Alexander Nevsky Lavra only. If you don't mind an early start, the **Smolny Cathedral** (services at 7am, 10am and 6pm, closed 2–5pm) is one of the most breathtakingly beautiful buildings in the city and can be seen on the way to the Lavra. A former museum, it is now used for choral concerts and art exhibitions. (If you're interested, find out about tickets inside.) You may have seen the cathedral against the skyline: painted pale blue and white, it seems to float rather than stand on the horizon. A ticket will take you on a climb inside the building, giving wonderful panoramic views of the city.

Smolny means tar and it seems somewhat incongruous that the site of such a cathedral was a tar yard until 1723. Peter's daughter, Tsarina Elizabeth, decided to build a convent there in 1744 and hired Bartolomeo Rastrelli, who later fell out of favour with Catherine II's preference for classicism. It was not completed until 39 years after Catherine's death in 1835, when Tsar Nicholas I commissioned the architect Vasily Stasov to add several new structures, converting it into a convent 'for the education of well-born young ladies', the first establishment of its kind in Russia.

At the beginning of the 18th century the **Smolny Institute** moved to the yellow, classical building next door, designed by Giacomo Quarenghi in 1808. This was to become the headquarters of the Bolshevik Central Committee, and it was from here that Lenin led the uprising in October 1917.

The Alexander Nevsky Lavra is situated on **Ploshchad Alexandra Nevskovo**, just opposite the metro station of the same name. From Smolny, take

a taxi to Ploshchad Alexandra Nevskovo or ask for the Hotel Moskva. Coming by metro you will find Hotel Moskva where you can stop for a coffee next door to the metro exit. You will also see the yellow archway into the *lavra* on the other side of the square.

The Alexander Nevsky

The oldest and most beautiful monastery complex in the city, the **Alexander Nevsky Lavra** is named after the Russian prince who saved the city from the Swedes in the 13th century and who was later canonised. His remains were brought here by Peter the Great in a silver coffin, which was then moved to the Hermitage.

It is perfectly acceptable to walk into the monastery when a service is being held and many people seem to come and go in this way, even worshippers. Don't be surprised if you see a baptism, a wedding and an open coffin all in one morning.

Lavra is a title bestowed upon a monastery of the highest order, the seat of Metropolitans, and before the Revolution there were only four in Russia – Kievo-Pecherskaya, Troitse-Sergieva (in Moscow), Pochayevskaya and this one. The Alexander Nevsky became a *lavra* in 1797 although it was founded by Peter the Great in 1713 – his sister Natalya Alexeyevna is buried here. The monastery was enlarged under Peter's successors, and the Holy Trinity Cathedral was built during the reign of Catherine II by one of her favoured architects, Ivan Starov.

The *lavra* is still a burial ground for famous people – 'there's a long queue' I was told by one of the attendants. Recently, Anna Akhmatova's son, Lev Gumilev, was buried here, as was Georgy Tovstonogov, one of the best-known contemporary theatre directors. There are several cemeteries inside the complex (Fri–Wed 10am–7pm, 4pm in winter). Some interesting headstones can be seen in the central courtyard outside, among them an aeroplane propeller that marks the grave of a pilot who was killed in World War II.

Most interesting of all are the two cemeteries, **Tikhvin** and **Lazarus**, which lie directly to the left and right of the gates as you enter the monastery. You have to

Left: mass at Holy Trinity Cathedral
Above: Rimsky-Korsakov's grave

F.E. Dzerzinskom
Smolny monastyr
Smolny sobor
Shpalernaya ul.
Tavricheskaya ul.
Tavrichesky dvoretz
Koncertno-Vystavochny kompleks
Smolny Insitut
Smolninskaya nab.
Muzey-kvartira Kozlova
most Petra Velikova
Tavricheskaya
Voenno-istorichesky muzey im. Suvorova
Suvorovsky prospekt
Tulskaya ul.
SMOLNINSKY RAYON
Krasnogvardeysky prosp.
ul. Moiseyenko
Novgorodskaya
8 Sovetskaya ul.
Muzey-kvartira Lenina
Neva
Sinopskaya nab.
Malookhtinsky prospekt
Muzey-kvartira Lenina
prosp. Bakunina
KRASNOG VARDEYSKAYA
Khersonskaya ul.
Zanevsky prosp.
most Al. Nevskovo
Nevsky prospekt
Hotel Moskva
PL. ALEKSANDRA NEVSKOVO
Sinopskaya nab.
Itinerary 5
Muzey gorodskoy skulptury
Svyato-Troicky sobor
Aleksandro-Nevskaya lavra
Nevsky Lavra
750 m / 775 yds

pay to enter and tickets can be purchased at the gates. To the left is the Lazarus Cemetery where Peter the Great's sister is buried. There are also many important architects buried in the cemetery, such as Giacomo Quarenghi (the Manege, the Hermitage Theatre), Andreyan Zakharov (the Admiralty), Carlo Rossi (Russian Museum, General Staff Headquarters in Palace Square and the Alexandrinsky Theatre) and Andrei Voronikhin (the Kazan Cathedral).

To your right is the Tikhvin Cemetery, the burial site of famous composers such as Mikhail Glinka, Pyotr Tchaikovsky, Modest Mussorgsky and Nikolai Rimsky-Korsakov. Here also lies Fyodor Dostoevsky and the sculptor Pyotr Klodt, who created the horses on Anichkov Bridge.

The **Church of the Annunciation**, to the left of the main entrance, was built in 1717–22 by Domenico Trezzini. General Suvorov, Imperial Russia's most prominent military leader, is buried here. The beautiful **Holy Trinity Cathedral**, built by Ivan Starov, is inside the main complex with the Metropolitan House situated opposite. The cathedral, a later addition to the monastery, has to be the most European of St Petersburg's churches.

6. THE SPIT OF VASILIEVSKY ISLAND (see map, p43)

The Sphinxes, Menshikov Palace, the Kunstkamera and a choice of places for lunch.

Taxi to Most Lieutenant Schmidt (Vasilievsky Island side) or take the trolley bus No. 10 north from Nevsky Prospekt, or the metro to Vasileostrovskaya, followed by bus Nos 6 or 47.

This walk begins on Vasilievsky Ostrov (Island) by the statues of the **Egyptian Sphinxes** on Universitetskaya Naberezhnaya – University Embankment. The streets in this part of town are marked by academic disciplines and divided into grids. The Sphinxes date from the 13th century BC and were brought from Thebes in 1832. The long granite pier on which they stand is directly in front of the austere **Academy of Arts** (the arts university; museum open Wed–Su 11am–6pm), created in 1757. The Academy's collection includes works of art from the Soviet School of painting.

With the river to your right, walk past the **Obelisk**, which commemorates the Russian victories over the Turks under 18th-century Field Marshal, Rumyantsev, and the next building is the **Menshikov Palace** (Tues–Sun 10.30am–4.30pm), one of the city's first stone residences, built in the time of Peter the Great. Alexander Menshikov, a life-long friend of Peter's, built some splendid palaces. He was the city's first governor-general and head of the military department. Peter gave him Vasilievsky Island in 1707, and he had already built the palace before Peter took

Left: prow on a pillar
Above Right: Sphinx Quay

back his gift in 1714 in order to realise plans to make the island the nucleus of his new capital. However, the builders were defeated by the swampy soil and the plan came to naught. Before Peter built his own palaces, this one was used for entertaining guests. It is one of the few buildings whose early interior is still intact.

Peter the Great's Ministries

Leaving the palace, turn left, past two 18th-century buildings, and you come to the terracotta structure called the Twelve Colleges, part of **St Petersburg University**. The building, which stretches to your left down Mendeleyevskaya Linia, is one of the oldest in the city, first built by Peter the Great to house his *Kollegia* or ministries. Its architect gained the commission by winning of one of Russia's first building competitions. If you want to have a look inside, it is unlikely anyone will stop you; the entrance is on Mendeleyevskaya Linia.

Back on the Universitetskaya Naberezhnaya, the next building is the Academy of Sciences, created when the building next door, the Kunstkamera, became too crowded. For a further insight into the man who built this city, look at his Chamber of Curiosities in the Kunstkamera Museum of Anthro-

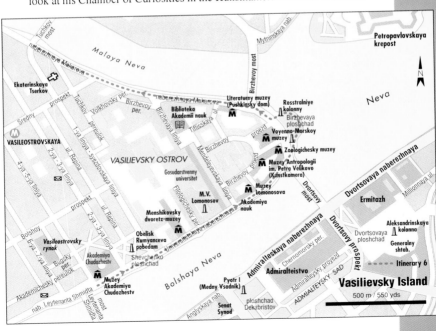

pology and Ethnography; (open Thur–Tues 10am– 5pm, closed last Thur in the month) – the blue and white building with the tower. The entrance is down the side street before the main building to your left, Tamozhenny Pereulok. The 'curiosities', on the ground floor under the dome, include embryos and human organs. The Kunstkamera also houses the museum of the Russian scholar Mikhail Lomonosov (1711–65).

With the Kunstkamera behind you, follow the embankment until you come to the main road, with the Dvortsovy (Palace) Bridge on your right. Turn left and keep walking, with the two **rostral columns** now in sight. The magnificent building dominating the 'spit' is the **Central Naval Museum** (open Wed–Sun 10.30am–4.45pm, closed last Thur in the month), the Stock Exchange before the Revolution. Until the 1880s this point of Vasilievsky Island was St Petersburg's main port. The red pillars were originally the light signals. They are decorated with the prows of boats which represent four great Russian rivers: the Volga, Dnieper, Neva and Volkhov.

If you have time, walk round the spit of the island, where you will often see newlyweds posing for photographs. Continue along the Makarov embankment with the Malaya Neva on your right. Just across Stock Exchange Bridge, on the Petrograd side, is a three-storey, floating plexi-glass barge. This is **Akvarel**, an upscale restaurant and club (the food in the bistro on the top floor is cheaper and the view is better). Another option is **Academia**, in the basement of the old Customs House behind the former Stock Exchange at Birzhevoi Proezd 1. The brick-oven pizza here is good, as is the atmosphere.

7. UP THE NEVSKY TO THE ANICHKOV BRIDGE *(see pullout map)*

Traditional icecreams, market stalls, the Kazan Cathedral and the art -nouveau House of Books.

Taxi to Admiralteistvo, or metro to Nevsky Prospekt. Nevsky Prospekt is 4.5 km (2.5 miles) long. This walk covers the first 2 km (1 mile).

Nevsky Prospekt is the very heart and soul of St Petersburg, integral to the city's very identity. As the city's main street, it is also its busiest and most colourful. Here you will find everything, from the best shopping and dining, to the leading hotels and some famous historical landmarks.

Where you stand, at the beginning of the **Nevsky Prospekt**, with the **Admiralty** and **Palace Square** behind you, there was once a forest. After the first Admiralty was built in 1705, a path had to be cleared through it to link the ship-building yard with the town of Novgorod. People built houses and palaces along it, and called it the Nevsky Prospekt.

At the beginning, the Nevsky seems like any old street, but as you continue walking it widens and to your right and left huge squares open out, giving it a sense of space. It is also 'aired' by three waterways, the

Above: vintage store sign
Right: scenes on the steps of Kazan Cathedral

Moika, the **Griboedova** and the **Fontanka**.

The Nevsky is famous for icecreams, bought from kiosks on the street (numerous in areas popular with tourists) – the best ones come in wafer tubs and the prices vary according to flavour, which is usually vanilla, but you sometimes find crême brûlée or a fruit flavour. Some visitors prefer Russian icecreams for their home-made flavour, others will go for the more Western varieties as they can look more appealing and there are plenty of them to choose from.

The first important street you come to on your right will be **Malaya Morskaya Ulitsa**, previously named Ulitsa Gogolya after the writer Gogol, who lived at No. 17. Tchaikovsky died here, at No. 8. The next crossroads is the once-fashionable **Bolshaya Morskaya Ulitsa**, home of the famous Fabergé shop (No 24, to the right). It is still a jeweller's, but unfortunately has lost its former glory.

Home of the Stroganovs

The first river you come to is the **Moika** and on the right-hand side after the bridge stands the green-and-white **Stroganov Palace**, now a branch of the Russian Museum. The Stroganovs were one of Russia's most powerful and richest aristocratic families, and gave their name to the dish, beef Stroganov. The palace houses special exhibits from the Russian Museum collection, as well as visiting shows of works by important international artists. In the courtyard is the Stroganov Gardens Café, a nice quiet place to relax in the centre.

city itineraries

After the Palace, walk past **Bolshaya Konushennaya Ulitsa**, on your left, where Turgenev, and later Nijinsky, lived at No. 13. Rimsky-Korsakov lived at No. 11. Further on to the right you will see the huge **Kazan Cathedral** with 96 columns designed by the architect Andrei Voronikhin during and after the reign of Paul I. In the square in front of it are statues of the heroes of the 1812 war, Mikhail Kutuzov and Mikhail Barklay de Tolly. It once housed the Museum of the History of Religion and Atheism, but now the **Museum of Religion** has moved to Pochtamskaya Ulitsa.

Opposite, at No. 28, is the art-nouveau **Dom Knigi** (House of Books), once offices of the Singer Sewing Machine Company. A huge globe on the roof can be seen from afar. Try going up to the second floor, where you can often buy interesting maps and posters. As you turn left out of here and cross the bridge over the **Griboedova Canal** you will see to your left the multi-coloured domes of the **Church of Our Saviour on Spilled Blood** or **Church of the Resurrection** *(see page 26)*, built on the spot where Alexander II was assassinated.

This church was under restoration for some 25 years and has now emerged beautifully from its cocoon. Further up the Nevsky on the left, on the corner of Mikhailovskaya Ulitsa, is the yellow facade of the **Grand Hotel Europe**. Mikhailovskaya Ulitsa leads into **Ploshchad Iskusstv**, home of the Russian Museum.

You could stop at the Grand Hotel Europe for coffee or tea (entrance on Mikhailovskaya Ulitsa). I would suggest the bar to your left as you go in, or the **Sadkos** bar, which has its own entrance after the corner with Nevsky Prospekt. If it is after midday, there is a coffee shop a few metres up from the Grand Hotel Europe called **Nevsky 40** (open noon–midnight). There are numerous coffee shops on Nevsky. The yellow facade of **Gostinny Dvor** is opposite Nevsky 40, a department store selling all sorts of interesting curiosities.

As you leave Gostinny Dvor you will pass through an underpass, opposite which, at No. 56, is a once-famous food shop called **Elyseev's**. The Elyseev brothers were wealthy merchants and the extravagance of the shop's design makes it well worth a look.

Music, Theatre and Dance

On your right is a huge square with a statue of Catherine the Great and her closest state advisors and ministers. This is **Ploshchad Ostrovskovo**, laid out by the architect Carlo Rossi in the 1820s and 1830s, and named after Alexander Ostrovsky (1823–86), a playwright who wrote about the bourgeoisie. Take a little detour here and walk through the square, where you may see men playing chess. To your right is the **Russian National Library**. Through the trees you will also see the white columns of the **Pushkin Theatre of Drama**, known more familiarly as the Alexandrinsky.

Above: *Horse Tamers* on Anchikov bridge

Behind the theatre, on the left-hand corner of the square and Rossi Street stands the **Museum of Theatrical and Musical Art** (open Thur–Mon 11am–6pm, Wed 1–7pm, closed last Friday of the month). As you come out of here, turn left, then left again down **Ulitsa Zodchevo Rossi** – the street of the Master Builder Rossi, with its perfect proportions: the width of the street equals the height of the buildings. Rossi designed many yellow buildings in the city, such as the General Staff Headquarters in Palace Square and the Russian Museum (Mikhailovsky Palace).

On the left-hand side of this street is the **Vaganova Ballet School** where many famous Russian dancers trained, including Pavlova, Nijinsky and, much later in the 20th century, Nureyev, Makarova and Baryshnikov. Go back to the Nevsky and, keeping to the right, walk along it until you see the **Anichkov Bridge** with the dark red **Beloselsky-Belozersky Palace** behind.

The horses that decorate the Anichkov Bridge were designed by the sculptor Pyotr Klodt. His initial plan for the bridge – four groups of horses, two of them identical – was never realised as Nicholas I insisted on giving one of each pair away, the first to the King of Prussia, the second to the King of Naples. Luckily, Klodt's subsequent plan to prepare two new sculptures was accepted, and thus there are the four different statues that we can see today.

Good restaurants for lunch can be found in Karavannaya Ulitsa. Try **Mama Roma** at No. 3 or **Cat**, opposite at No. 24. For excellent Italian food there is **Milano** at No. 8, serving pasta and pizza dishes in an elegant setting at reasonable prices.

Above: elegant interior at Elyseev's
Right: down Nevsky Prospekt

8. LITERARY TOUR *(see pullout map)*

This tour visits the museums dedicated to some of Russia's most revered writers, including Dostoevsky, Pushkin and Nabokov.

Begin at Vladimirskaya metro station.

St Petersburg belongs to the small number of world capitals that have acted as rich sources of inspiration for their writers. But probably no other city in the world has such high regard and affection for its writers as St Petersburg. Indeed, writers are national heroes in Russia, especially in this city where many of the greatest lived and wrote.

Despite the freezing winter temperatures, hundreds of local people queue up outside the last residence of the poet Alexander Pushkin to pay tribute on the anniversary of the day he was killed in a duel with a Frenchman. Many ordinary Russians can quote Pushkin's work, and that of other writers, at great length. If you want to make a favourable impression on Russians, you can do no better than to learn their literature and everything tied to it; and if you can learn to read in the original Russian, you will win the highest level of respect.

The Great Dostoevsky

The city has a number of 'flat museums' dedicated to writers, as well as monuments. Perhaps the Russian writer best known to foreigners is Dostoevsky, so the best place to start a literary tour is at the **Feodor Dostoevsky Apartment-Museum** (Kuznechny Pereulok 5; Tues–Sun

11am–6pm, closed the last Wed of the month). Dostoevsky lived in this small apartment from 1878 to 1881 – a record for him since in 28 years he lived in more than 20 different places. The lives of his characters often derived from his own experiences and surroundings, and sometimes 'lived' in the same apartment as him. It is highly recommended that you take the museum's offer of a tour of city locations connected to the writer's stories.

Down the street from the museum, by the entrance to the Vladimirskaya metro station, is a recent monument to the writer.

The **Anna Akhmatova Museum** (Fontanka 34; Tues–Sun 11am–6pm, closed the last Wed of the month), in the back of the Sheremetev Palace, opened in 1989 on the 100th anniversary of the poet's birth. This is where one of Russia's greatest 20th-century poets spent most of her life. The museum has many of her manuscripts and about 13,500 items of memorabilia, as well as numerous paintings.

Above: *Anna Akhamatova* by Natan Altmann, 1914

Now head back to Nevsky Prospekt and go towards the Hermitage. Along the way, stop at the **Mikhail Zoshchenko Museum** (Malaya Konnushennaya 4/2, Flat 119; Tues–Sun 10.30am–6 .30pm, closed the last Wed of the month). This influential Soviet writer's satire on life during Stalin's time led to him being booted out of the Writers' Union.

Turn the corner and check out the monument to leading 19th-century writer, **Nikolai Gogol**, on Malaya Konnushennaya. A few kilometres from this statue is another, **The Nose**, located on a building on the corner of Ulitsa Rimsky-Korsakova and Voznesensky Prospekt. The Nose was the hero of one of Gogol's fantastic short stories, which features a nose wandering around St Petersburg.

Beloved Pushkin

Alexander Pushkin is revered as Russia's greatest writer. The **All-Russian Pushkin Museum** has three branches in the city and its suburbs (all Wed–Mon10.30am–5pm, closed the last Fri of the month). The **Alexander Pushkin–Museum** is the easiest to get to, and the best one to visit if time is limited (Naberezhnaya Reki Moki 12). In the suburb of Pushkin, the other two museums are the **Pushkin Lyceum Museum** (Sadovaya Ulitsa 2) and the **Pushkin Dacha Museum** (Pushkinsaya Ulitsa 2).

As you head to St Isaac's Square, you will see on the facade of the Angleterre Hotel, on the side bordering Bolshaya Morskaya, a memorial plaque to popular poet **Sergei Yesenin**, the so-called 'Last Poet of the Village'. He hanged himself – some would say he was forced to by the Soviet secret police – in the hotel in 1925.

Go across St Isaac's Square, and at Bolshaya Morskaya Ulitsa 47, you will find the **Vladimir Nabokov Museum** (Tues–Sun 11am–6pm), in the house inhabited by his family before they emigrated in 1917. Nabokov, who mostly lived in Europe and the United States, and is most famous for his novel *Lolita*, said that this was his 'only home in the world'. The first floor houses the museum: although the collection is not extensive, it continues to grow as people make donations

Although few foreigners have read Alexander Blok, he is considered one of the greatest poets of Russia's Silver Age in the early 20th century. The **Alexander Blok Museum** (Ulitsa Dekabristov 57; Thur–Tues 11am–5pm, closed the last Tues of the month) is in the house where the writer lived from 1912 until his death in 1921, when the country was ravaged by civil war and famine. There are numerous personal belongings, books and photographs.

Above: Pushkin outside the Russian Museum

9. PISKAROVSKOYE MEMORIAL CEMETERY *(see pullout map)*
The cemetery for the victims of the Leningrad Blockade.

Taxi to Piskarovskoye Kladbische.

If you arrived in St Petersburg by air, you will have passed the impressive monument to the **Heroes of the Defence of Leningrad** during World War II, in Ploshchad Pobedy (Victory Square) on the way in from the airport. Another, perhaps more important, tribute is the **Piskarovskoye Memorial Ceme-**

tery on the outskirts of the city. It is not easy to reach by public transport, so it is best to take a taxi. Although a visit to a cemetery may seem like a grim day out, it offers a fascinating account of a devastating episode in the city's history.

The Siege of Leningrad
The Germans invaded Russia in July 1941 and reached Leningrad in August. The city was encircled and cut off by road and by rail from September, when mass bombing began. Only a tiny tract of land on the shores of Lake Ladoga remained unoccupied by the enemy. When the narrower part of the lake froze, a 37-km (23-mile) ice road – the Road of Life – was laid, but this did not bring enough food for the city and by November the threat of famine was real. The bread ration was 250 grams (9 oz) a day for workers, 125 grams (4.5 oz) for others. There was no electricity, and by December no water supply or public transport, either.

Soviet troops broke through the blockade in January 1943 and provisions reached the city through the Finland Station. The Germans were finally defeated in the Leningrad region in January 1944. By this time, some 16,000 civilians had been killed by air raids and heavy shelling, and over 33,000 had been wounded. Hundreds of thousands more lives were lost through starvation. But everyone carried on working – factory workers continued to supply new and repaired tanks and ammunition, scientists researched new explosives from natural resources, Vavilov's famous Plant Breeding Institute remained intact – musicians even went on composing. Dmitri Shostakovich's *Seventh (Leningrad) Symphony* was broadcast on all wavelengths in 1942 from the Leningrad Philharmonia in Ploshchad Iskusstv.

The mass graves of 470,000 victims of the blockade line the long central alley. Civilian graves are marked by a hammer and sickle, military ones by a star. Two rooms by the entrance chart the history of the siege, step by step, with excellent black and white photographic evidence and the famous document of a young girl's diary – each entry records the death of another member of her family, ending with the words 'They have all died'.

Above: cemetery memorial

10. MOIKA BOAT TRIP AND BATHS *(see map, p53)*

A sightseeing boat trip where you can plan your own route, and a visit to a traditional Russian steam bath.

Metro to Nevsky Prospekt. Trips (summer only) start where the Nevsky Prospekt crosses over the Moika Canal.

Peter the Great loved Amsterdam and the existing canals in St Petersburg were adapted in an attempt to emulate the Dutch city. Two kinds of boats go up the canals – the long river boats that seat numerous passengers and the smaller taxi-boats that seat from two to 10 people. We are going to catch a taxi-boat. You will see signs for these on the Nevsky Prospekt as it crosses over the Moika. These boats literally operate as taxis so you have to catch one when it is free. The tours are obviously more popular in the summer months, and cannot run in the depth of winter when the canals freeze up, but there is no fixed time in the year when they start or stop – everything depends on the weather. It is impossible to give an approximate price – the boatman will suggest a price which will probably sound too much, so it is worth bargaining. Pay what you would think reasonable in Europe or the USA, remembering that each tour lasts an hour, and that this is one of the best and most relaxing ways to see the city.

The taxi-boats do not have a fixed route, so you can show the boatman the way you want to go by pointing at a map. (He will have one, but you may like to take your own, just in case.) I would suggest the following – Moika River to New Holland, Kriukov Canal, Griboedova Canal, join the Fontanka by the Summer Gardens, out into the Neva, turn left until you reach the Hermitage where you turn left again into a canal that takes you back to the Moika.

Above: the Red Bridge
Right: the Blue Bridge

Highlights on the Moika

It is impossible to name each building you pass or each bridge you go under, but look out for the following: the first building on your left after the Nevsky crosses the Moika is the green-and-white **Stroganov Palace**. Further on to the left is a former orphanage at No. 48, now one of the buildings forming the **Herzen Pedagogical Institute**. Count one bridge and you then approach **St Isaac's Square** and the statue of Nicholas I. To your left is the **Mariinsky Palace**, built in 1839–40 by Andrey Stakensshneider, and presented by Nicholas I to his daughter Maria. It is now the seat of the city legislature, and was heavily defended by barricades and crowds during the August 1991 abortive coup against Gorbachev's government. The bridge under which you pass at this point, the Blue Bridge (its original colour when it was wooden) is the widest in the city.

Further along on the left at No. 94 stands the **Yusupov Palace**, home of the chief assassin of Rasputin, who was murdered here in 1916. This museum is worth visiting another time. Further along on the right, where the boat will turn to the left up the Kriukov Canal, is the red-brick -**New Holland**, where Peter the Great stored his ship-building timber. The next important building on the left is the pale green **Mariinsky Theatre**, which backs onto the river. Maria, from whom the theatre takes its name, was the wife of Alexander II.

You will not be able to miss the sparkling domes of the **St Nicholas'** or

Sailors' Cathedral, first the bell tower by the river, and then as you turn the corner into the Griboedova Canal, the church itself. It was built between 1753–62 by Savva Chevakinsky. The canal bends round and you go under the **Lion Bridge**. When the canal forms its next bend, to your right is a famous Dostoevsky setting. **Sennaya Ploshchad**, the former Haymarket, was featured in *Crime and Punishment*. Further on is the spectacular **Bank Bridge** on which sit some sculpted griffins. According to ancient Greek mythology, griffins guard gold, and here they stand guard over the former State Bank, which is located directly to the right and is now the University of Finance and Economics.

Immediately afterwards comes the **Kazan Cathedral** and you now pass under the Nevsky Prospekt again, heading for the striking, onion-domed church that looms at the end of the canal, the **Church of Our Saviour on Spilled Blood (Church of the Resurrection**, *see page 26*). Before you reach this, to your right is the yellow Benois Wing of the Russian Museum. You can now see the church close up, in all its splendour.

After the church, the boat should bear right, with the **Field of Mars** on your left, and the **Mikhailovsky (Russian Museum) Gardens** on your right. The next splendid sight you will see is the terracotta-red **Mikhailovsky**

Above: exploring by canal
Above right: Sailors' Cathedral

Castle, which looks more like a fortress. It was here that Tsar Paul I was assassinated by nobles who supported the ascension of his son, Alexander, to the throne. Some 20 years later it became a Military Engineering Academy. The entrance to the Summer Gardens is just opposite it. You now come to the Fontanka Canal and take a left turn towards what seems like the open sea. Just before you come to the Neva, the small yellow house to your left is Peter the Great's **Summer Palace** *(see page 30)*.

The boat should turn left past the gates to the Summer Gardens. Go under Troitsky Bridge with the Field of Mars to the left and the statue of the great General Suvorov, a hero of the campaign against Napoleon. The **Field of Mars**, a former marsh, then a parade ground, was redesigned and landscaped after the Revolution by the architect Lev Rudnev. It is claimed that the bodies of some of those killed in the Revolution are buried here, but historians have doubts as to who they were and what they did. Most are believed to be people killed in street clashes between 1917 and 1919. An eternal flame, created in 1957, burns in the centre, commemorating the victims. This square is beautiful on a summer evening and is popular with

city itineraries

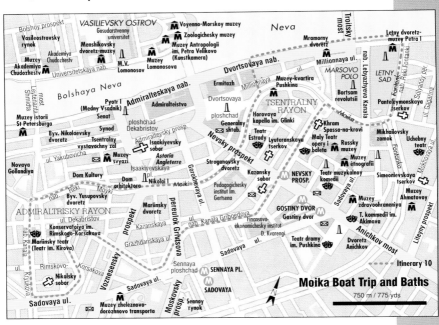

Moika Boat Trip and Baths

750 m / 775 yds

- - - Itinerary 10

local people and tourists alike. Directly after this is the **Marble Palace**. You will now have an incredible view of the city.

Your water-taxi will now turn left under a little bridge, with the **Hermitage** buildings on your right and the Hermitage Theatre on your left and sail up the Zimnaya Kanavka, the Winter Canal, until it meets up with the Moika River where you take a right turn and go under the **Pevchesky (Choristers')** **Bridge**. After the bridge on the left is the St Petersburg State Capella Hall, once the home of the Court Choir. You should now be heading back towards the bridge and your point of disembarkation.

Time to Steam

It is an old Russian tradition to take a **steam bath** and the one I recommend is situated just off Nevsky Prospekt at Ulitsa Marata 5/7, tel: 311-1400 (metro stop: Mayakovskaya or Ploshchad Vosstaniya). Most hotels have their own steam rooms and saunas (the Grand Hotel Europe offers a luxurious experience with saunas, jacuzzis and massage facilities), but if you want to experience the genuine article, visit this traditional establishment.

You should be sure to come equipped with your own soap, something to cover your head – a bath hat if you have one, but Russian women often wear woollen hats – and your own flip-flops, if possible; you are given a towel on arrival which looks more like a white sheet. Most important of all, for traditional bathers, is a bundle of birch or oak branches – but they won't turn you away if you don't have one. Often, individual vendors will offer these for sale outside the door to the baths.

Don't expect luxury, although you should ask for 'luxe' when you go in. There will be an attendant with whom you leave your bags and hire a towel, etc. Sometimes you can arrange to have a massage as well. You pay at the end of your visit. Inside you will find a steam room, a sauna and a small, freezing-cold swimming pool, together with showers. It all looks pretty basic and old-fashioned, but it is well worth the experience.

Above: snacks in the *banya*
Right: Church of Our Saviour on the Spilled Blood

Excursions

1. PETRODVORETZ – PETER'S PALACE   *(see pullout map)*

A boat or train trip to the most important of the palaces outside St Petersburg. Take food and drink with you.

Take a hydrofoil from the pier outside the Hermitage on Dvortsovaya Naberezhnaya or take a train from Baltic Station (metro station Baltiiskaya) to Novy Peterhof.

If you are only in St Petersburg for a limited time, it can be difficult deciding which palace to visit – that is, if you are allowed to choose for yourself. Of all the palaces open to the public, **Petrodvoretz** (main palace open Tuesday–Sunday 10.30am–5pm, closed the last Tuesday of the month; tel: 420-0073 for further information), located 29 km (18 miles) west of the city, on the Gulf of Finland, is considered to be the most impressive. One of the advantages of travelling under your own steam is that you can leave your choices until the last minute. A great deal depends on the weather and the time of year. It is fun to take the hydrofoil boat there in the summer months, but a ride on the electric railway can also be an adventure, and you will certainly feel less like a tourist.

The most striking feature of Petrodvoretz is its magnificent fountains but in the winter these are turned off. The splendid Lion's Cascading Fountain was switched on again in August 2000, after extensive restoration work meant it was out of action for five years.

In the summer, usually between May and September, you can take a hydrofoil boat to Petrodvoretz from the embankment in front of the Hermitage. Here you buy tickets one way only. The return tickets are sold at the pier at Petrodvoretz and it is usually best to purchase them on arrival, to ensure you have a place on the way back. Boats leave St Petersburg every 45 minutes from 9am–6.30pm and take you all the way.

The palace at Petrodvoretz was built by Peter the Great in 1720 to the design of a French architect, Jean Baptiste Le Blond, who, like so many architects, did not live to supervise the construction of his scheme. The original palace was much simpler than the one you see today, which was enlarged and embellished by Peter's daughter, Elizabeth, but through the baroque glitz, traces of its founder and architect show through. The Palace has a magnificent site on a natural slope of ground – a Versailles by the sea – and intricate fountains which were a major feat of engineering as the land consists of marshy clay.

If you look at old pictures of Petrodvoretz, taken after World War II, you wonder how architects ever

Left: Peterhof piano and portraits
Right: Peterhof fountain detail

rebuilt it. The scene after the German occupation was one of utter devastation. Some, but by no means all, of the treasures were evacuated to safety in time.

If you have come by boat and are walking up from the shore, you will see the **Grand Cascade** fountains – the focal point of the Water Gardens – as you approach the Palace. Completed in 1724, the elaborate bronze fountain, with the famous **statue of Samson** rending apart the jaws of a lion, was also designed by Le Blond and was intended as a symbolic celebration of Russia's victory over the Swedes.

The ticket offices, КACCA, are located at the back of the palace. Tourists are given priority over locals here when it comes to being allowed in, although they have to pay more.

Put on your *tapochki* (slippers) and set off, either listening to a tour narrated in your own language, or on your own. If you want to study the palace in detail, there are books and leaflets on sale. Don't miss the **Oak Staircase** and **Oak Study**, which reflect Peter the Great's taste. Some of the darker oak panels, designed by Nicholas Pineau, are the originals; also see the **Portrait Gallery** of 368 women in different costumes, which Catherine introduced, and the **Throne Room**, where Peter's original throne sits.

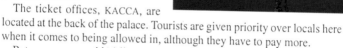

If you come here in summer, try not to leave without seeing the three pavilions in the gardens (all three are closed during the winter months). The first, the **Hermitage**, was where Peter entertained his guests and a dumb waiter device operated, as a section of the round table was lowered to be cleared and replenished below. The **Marly** is built in a simple, Dutch style, and **Monplaisir**, by the water's edge, came to be Peter's favourite retreat – he could watch the sea from his bed. Marly is closed on Monday, Monplaisir and the Hermitage are both closed on Thursday, but all are open at the weekend.

If you take a walk behind the palace to the upper garden you will discover the **Peterhof Palace Pharmacy** where you can try different herbal drinks concocted to cure all manner of ailments.

Above: Peterhof. **Left:** Grand Cascade fountains
Right: Oranienbaum's Chinese Palace

2. ORANIENBAUM *(see pullout map)*

A summer trip to a royal palace that escaped the German bombs.

Take a train from Baltic Station (metro: Baltiiskaya) to the Lomonosov Station.

The Oranienbaum Palace ensemble covers 165 hectares (408 acres) on the Gulf of Finland, some 40 km (24 miles) southwest of St Petersburg. It includes 53 historic buildings, of which 18 are federally protected. It is only 12 km (7 miles) down the coast from Petrodvoretz, so, at a stretch, the two could be combined (the station is on the same line). The palace ensemble is divided into several parts: the Lower Park and Main Palace, Peter III's City, the Upper Park, Sliding Hill and the Chinese Palace.

Oranienbaum (park open daily 9am–10pm; palace and museums Wed–Mon 11am–5pm, closed last Mon of the month) has only recently opened some of its rooms to the public. Its most impressive site is the Chinese Palace, which is on the World Monuments Fund list of top 100 endangered sites. Oranienbaum was St Petersburg's only major historical landmark to escape destruction during World War II, as Soviet troops held out against German encirclement, but subsequent decades of neglect took their toll.

In 1707, Peter the Great gave the land here to his close friend and advisor, Prince Alexander Menshikov. Construction on the **Grand (Menshikov) Palace** began in 1711 and lasted until 1727 when Menshikov fell from power and was exiled, just two years after Peter's death. The prince planted orange trees here, hence the name Oranienbaum, which means orange tree in German, a language considered fashionable at Peter's Europhile court. Architects Fontana and Shedel supervised the main palace's construction, and connected it to the Gulf of Finland with a canal, which has not survived. They also built the Lower Park, and decorated it with fountains and sculptures, as well as building parts of the Upper Park. Prince Menshikov spared no expense with Oranienbaum, which pretty much led to his financial ruin. It was partly out of friendly rivalry that Peter launched construction of the nearby, sumptuous Petrodvoretz.

In 1743 Peter's daughter, the Empress Elizabeth, gave Oranienbaum to her heir, the Grand Duke Peter Fedorovitch (future Emperor Peter III), for his summer residence. During Peter's 10-year residency, Rastrelli reconstructed the Grand Palace, giving it the exquisite appearance you see today. In the late 1750s, Peter built a small fort, the Petrstadt Fortress, which included a small 'palace' (in fact a small, two-storey building), and the Gate of Honour with a tower, surrounded by barracks, fortifications and a moat that were all torn down in the late 18th century. All that remain are the palace and gate.

Catherine the Great came to power in 1762 after deposing her husband, Peter III, who only served as Tsar for six months. From 1762–64, she had the Chinese Palace and the Katalnaya Gorka, or Roller-coaster Pavilion, built.

If you arrive by train, walk from the station towards the cathedral. Next to the entrance is the grave of the Russian émigré Prince George Galitzine, who spent most of his life in Britain. His mother was born and brought up in the Great Palace, and the last 30 years of his life were dedicated to encouraging Westerners to appreciate Russian culture. Now cross the road, and the entrance to the park is to your right.

Although not all of the main palace is open, it is interesting and atmospheric to see a splendid untouched and derelict building. But the fantastic Chinese Palace has much more to offer, and although parts of it have been slightly restored, it is the only original 18th-century palace in or near St Petersburg. The city government recently created a foundation to raise about US$90 million to rebuild Oranienbaum by the time of its 300th anniversary in 2011.

3. GULF OF FINLAND (see pullout map)

A day trip to the resort district of choice with St Petersburg residents.

Take the commuter train from the Finland Station to any town along the north shore of the Gulf of Finland, but allow for a 25-minute walk to the beach. Bus 213 from metro Chernaya Rechka drops you at the beach, but traffic may make it slow going. If possible, hire a car for the day.

Few travellers to St Petersburg make their way to the north shore of the Gulf of Finland, as it lacks the glittering tsarist palaces found on the southern shore. But a visit here will reveal a lesser-known, fun side of city life, and one with a truly local character.

The north shore is officially called the Resort District, and falls within the St Petersburg city limits. Geographically, the area is part of the Karelian Isthmus, but don't confuse it with Russia's Karelia Republic much further to the north. The Gulf's south shore was the summer watering hole for the tsarist elite before 1917, and the north shore first became a resort in the late 19th century when St Petersburg's growing class of

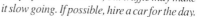

Left: moorings at the Gulf of Finland. **Right:** isolated, inland lakes make a tranquil getaway.

businessmen and intelligentsia chose to spend their summers here. A number of sanatoria sprang up to offer spa treatments. This shore is where today's wealthy Russians, and the not-so-wealthy intelligentsia, prefer to spend summer weekends.

For centuries, the Resort District was mostly populated by small Finnish villages, and even today many places bear Finnish names. When Lenin gave Finland its independence in 1918, the new border with the Soviet Union went through here. If you drive along the Primorskoye Shosse, look for the small, fortified positions to your left as you leave the village of Sestroretsk. These were the Soviet border posts before 1939, when the USSR invaded Finland and annexed a large part of the country.

The Resort District is easy to navigate by car since only one road from St Petersburg, the Primorskoye Shosse, heads that way. Shortly after leaving the city and passing the access ramp to the St Petersburg ring road, you will see a road on your left leading to the island of **Kotlin**. The island can be reached by driving across the flood protection barrier, a huge earthen dam that ranks as one of the largest engineering projects in Europe and stretches from the north to the south of the Gulf. Construction began in the early 1980s and completion is scheduled for 2010.

The city of **Kronshtadt** is on the island. Founded by Peter the Great in 1704 to defend St Petersburg from attack by sea, Kronshtadt later served as the city's main commercial port. Before the Revolution it was also the headquarters of the Russian Imperial Navy, and even in Soviet times it was an important naval base, closed to foreigners. The city only opened to outsiders in 1996, and can now be visited freely.

Kronshtadt is also known for the crushing of a sailors' mutiny during the so-called 1921 Kronshtadt Rebellion, which historians say was a major factor in convincing Lenin that the Russian people would not easily accept Soviet socialism. The result was the enactment of the New Economic Policy (NEP) that allowed for a brief return to capitalism and subsequent strong economic growth after years of decline and civil war.

Leaving the village of **Sestroretsk**, the Shosse forks into the Lower Primorsky Shosse, which runs along the water, and the Upper Primorsky

Shosse, which runs parallel, about 1 km (half a mile) inland. Once you get off these main roads, however, travelling is extremely difficult because directional signs are rare, and most roads are narrow and unsurfaced. However, this adds to the area's charm, as you feel transported back into a simpler, more tranquil era.

In the Soviet period, Sestroretsk and several of the other villages were famed for *dachas* belonging to the Communist Party elite and the intelligentsia, most of whom were in silent opposition to the regime, and who first colonised the area at the end of the 19th century. To get a glimpse of that era, visit the **Muzei Repina** (Repin Museum) in **Repino** (Primorskoye Shosse 411; open Wednesday–Monday 10.30am–5pm, till 4pm in winter; tel: 231-6828), about 50 km (32 miles) from the city.

Few foreigners know the great Russia painter, Ilya Repin (1844–1930), but Russians almost deify him. In the late 19th century he was a founding member of the first counter-culture art movement, the Wanderers *(Peredvizhniki)*, whose style came to resemble the French Impressionists. The *Peredvizhniki* rebelled against the classicism of the St Petersburg Academy of Arts and strove to create art that was more realistic and accessible to the masses. Most of Repin's works hang in the Russian Museum, but nearly 100 can be found here, where he spent the last 30 years of his life. His residence became a place of pilgrimage for Russian cultural figures, including poets Sergei Yesenin and Vladimir Mayakovsky and scientist Ivan Pavlov.

In Repino you will also find the best place to eat in the Resort District, **Shalyapin Restaurant and Nightclub**, Nagornaya Ulitsa (at the corner of Upper Primorskoye Shosse), tel: 231-6775. It has a modern and comfortable interior and serves Russian and international cuisine. Since it's about 1 km (half a mile) from the beach, prices are more reasonable. You will find it directly opposite Repino railway station.

The next town is **Komarovo**, in whose cemetery lies the poet Anna Akhmatova (1889–1966), and academic Dmitri Likhachev (1906–99), whose opposition to the Soviet regime and seminal work in Russian literature earned him the title, the Conscience of Russia. The avant-garde underground composer, Sergei Kuryokhin (1954–96), is also buried here.

The last town in the Resort District is **Zelenogorsk**, known by its Finnish name, Terijoki, before the Soviets conquered the region in 1939. Zelenogorsk has a beautiful, 19th-century Russian Orthodox church, built in the old style, and its fine beaches and outdoor cafés attract thousands in the summer.

Unfortunately the weather on the Gulf, even in summer, is often cool and windy, and there are few days warm enough to swim. But if weather permits, you can walk far into the sea through the shallow waters. At the very

Above: al fresco painting
Right: sunset on the Gulf of Finland

least, a walk on the beach, especially towards evening, is always romantic. Some places, such as the Golden Beach complex in Zelenogorsk, hire out windsurfing equipment, jet skis, and other water-sports equipment.

One of the best seaside locations, however, is the Resort District's first private beach, **High Dive**, in Komarovo. It has a small amusement park for children, several cafés, and boat and jet ski rental outlets. The finest feature, however, is its reputation as the cleanest beach on the Gulf.

For younger people, there are several nightclub and party scenes springing up on the beach. Next to High Dive is the **Jet Set Beach**, which is the outdoor party branch of the fashionable city nightclub of the same name. Jet Set Beach has clean, white sand – something no other beach can offer – and a good atmosphere. There's a small amusement park for children and the restaurant offers Japanese and Mediterranean food. The beach is open to members only, but foreign tourists get free admission if they call the Jet Set Club in St Petersburg (tel: 275-9288; www.jetset.spb.ru).

If you are not after laid-on entertainment and facilities, the lakes a little further inland are worth exploring, and the water there is often pristine.

Health Spas and Resorts

Among reputable spas on the Gulf are:

The Old Mill, Solnechnoe Village, 2nd Borovaya Ulitsa 16, tel: 437-1648; e-mail: old_mill@smtp.ru; www.oldmillvip.spb.ru. This health spa provides a wide range of services, including Russian baths and a Finnish sauna, as well as honey massages. On its premises are three fine restaurants.

Repino Sanatorium, Repino Village, Primorskoye Shosse 394, tel: 380-2131; e-mail: sales@repino.spb.ru; www.repino.spb.ru. A health spa that offers a wide range of bath treatments, as well as massage.

Dunes, Zelenorgorsk; Primorskoye Shosse, 38th Km, tel: 437-4438 or 437-4767; e-mail: dunes@golf.spb.ru ; www.golf.spb.ru. Dunes is the most prominent resort and health spa on the Gulf, mostly because, besides a wide range of treatments and baths, it has the only professional golf course in the region. Walks in its extensive pine forest are often prescribed for those suffering from respiratory ailments.

Leisure Activities

SHOPPING

St Petersburg is not traditionally regarded as a shopper's paradise, and high-priced imported goods have been squeezing out the local wares, but there are all sorts of interesting things you can buy here nevertheless. If it is souvenirs you want, you will have no trouble – it's not all *matreshkas* (nests of dolls). The city offers both the established department stores and a host of street-sellers with a diverse range of goods, including vodka, caviar and Russian toys *(see page 75 for customs information).*

With the market economy, there are stalls everywhere, particularly outside tourist haunts. Before you even get into the Peter and Paul Fortress, or wander around the Alexander Nevsky Monastery, you will be encouraged to spend, spend, spend.

Folk art predominates in the form of *palekh* and woodwork. *Palekh* used to be a school of icon painting and is now the word used to describe the intricate painting of enamelled wooden boxes. But far more widespread, and better value for money, are the hand-painted bowls, trays, wooden spoons, boxes, chess sets and rings from Khokhloma.

You can also find china, embroidered linens and jewellery, such as amber and malachite. When it comes to clothing, you can choose between furs, T-shirts and army uniforms – soldiers' hats, belts and coats. There are many lavish coffee-table books, printed in various languages. If it's trinkets you are seeking, there are endless badges, cigarette lighters and key rings. And you won't have to look very far to find a samovar or a balalaika (a three-stringed musical instrument). The image of Lenin lingers on, particularly on badges and old flags, but it is withering fast.

If you are an imaginative and adventurous shopper, then you should check out the Russian shops. Locals will often advise you to avoid street sellers, particularly when it comes to purchasing alcohol and food. But quality products such as knitwear can often be picked up on street stalls. In shops, the Russian system is to pay first at the till, then take your ticket to the cashier who will wrap up what you have bought. It's much cheaper to buy postcards in this way than in hotels. I have listed a selection of stores, but if you feel like browsing, the main shopping streets are the Nevsky, Kamennoostrovsky, Bolshoi and Liteiny prospekts.

The Russian customs regulations are unpredictable, ranging from extremely strict to incredibly lax. Some visitors to Russia tell you they managed to take a variety of items out of the country with no trouble whatsoever. Others will complain of how a beautiful old samovar or balalaika was confiscated by customs officials. What you have to be careful about are valuable antiques such as icons and paintings produced before 1945, and large amounts of caviar. (The machine that photographs your luggage as you leave the country is quick to pick up the fish logo on the tins.)

However, if you can prove that you have paid legally by showing your receipt, you should have no trouble taking out most items. It is wise to check with your tour operator on what is permitted at the time of your visit, as prices and laws can change rapidly.

Left: Gostiny Dvor
Right: typical Russian doll

Antiques

RUSSKAYA STARINA
Nevsky Prospekt 20
Open 11am–9pm, Sunday till 6pm.
Some of the city's finest antiques are on sale here, but they are pricy.

LOMANNY GROSH
Mokhovaya Ulitsa 31
Open 11am–8pm.
Specialises in Soviet-era antiques and curiosities.

LARUSSE
Stremyanaya Street 3
www.larusse.ru
Open 11am–8pm.
The world's only antique shop that specialises exclusively in rural Russian antiques. Friendly English-speaking staff will gladly provide a tour and explain all the items.

Gifts

ONEGIN ART STORE
Italyanskaya Ulitsa 11
www.onegin-art.com.
Open 9am–9pm.
Wide range of fine Russian handicrafts.

STROGANOV PALACE ART STORE
Nevsky Prospekt 17
Open 10am–8pm.
Wide selection of Russian souvenirs and folk items.

GRAND PALACE
Nevsky Prospekt 21–23
www.grand-palace.ru

Open 11am–9pm.
This is the city's most elite shopping mall.

PASSAGE
Nevsky Prospekt 48
Open 10am–9pm.
A 19th-century shopping arcade with fine souvenirs and other items.

Gourmet Food

YELISEYEVSKY GASTRONOM
Nevsky Prospekt 56
Open 10am–9pm.
Stocks fine delicacies; this is a great place to buy caviar.

YAKHONT
Bolshaya Morskaya Ulitsa 24
Open daily 10am–7pm, Sunday 11am–7pm.
Metro: Gostinny Dvor or Nevsky Prospekt.
Housed in the old Fabergé building, it sells a range of jewellery.

Shopping for Food

Good Russian bread can be bought at bakeries *(bulochnaya)* throughout the city. Here are some of the main fruit and vegetable markets (other goods, such as clothes, are also available at these markets):

KUZNECHNY RYNOK
Kuznechny Pereulok 3
Closed Monday.
Metro: Dostoevskaya or Vladimirskaya.

NEKRASOVSKY RYNOK
Nekrasova Ulitsa 52
Metro: Ploschad Vosstaniya.

Supermarkets

There is a good range of imported produce at the following:

KALINKA STOCKMANN
Finlandia Prospekt 1
Open 9am–10pm.
Metro: Ploshchad Lenina.

SUPERMARKET AT PASSAGE DEPARTMENT STORE
Nevsky Prospekt 48
Open 11am–9pm. Metro: Nevsky Prospekt.

Above: creative, yet traditional, window frames
Right: fine dining in St Petersburg

EATING OUT

Eating in Russia has certainly improved in the past 20 years, mostly since restaurants became privately owned in 1986. Gone are the days when there was little to choose between institutional Soviet canteens called *stolovayas* serving something like school food, or large, dark restaurants, which shut out the daylight and where, in the evening, it was hard to converse against an ear-shattering musical floor show.

These days you can see into most cafés and restaurants from the street, and menus are normally translated into English (French restaurants translate menus into French). Many chefs are trained abroad and there are many Western-owned and run enterprises, including internationally-known fast-food outlets.

It is hard to give an example of a traditional Russian meal, particularly now that there is so much foreign influence, but generally it takes the form of a feast or celebration, which for most Russians is best served at home. Russian home cooking is always best, especially if it includes the influence of Georgian cooking, which uses nuts, spices and vegetables such as aubergines, from the south.

Zakuski are starters and there are plenty of them, ranging from cold meat, pickled and salted fish, salads with sour cream (*smetana*) or mayonnaise dressings, to small portions of red (*keta*) or black (*ikra*) caviar, all served with plenty of black rye bread and the sweeter white pancakes (*blinis*). Then comes the soup course; either the traditional *bortsch* (beetroot) or *shchi*

(cabbage), then a meat dish followed by a sweet course (Russians tend to have a sweet tooth); the quality of cakes varies between the authentic and the synthetic.

Similarly, with the exception of vodka and beer, Russian drinks are on the sweet side, particularly the Georgian wines and champagne. *Sukhoye*, meaning 'dry', is a useful word when ordering drinks. Many Western brands of drinks are also widely available.

Some Russian bars can be dark, rough places where you may not feel comfortable. At the other end of the scale, expensive Western versions are proliferating.

The following restaurants, cafés and bars comprise a recommended selection from many in the city and, with a few exceptions, are centrally located. They are listed by category and price range. To avoid disappointment, it is safer to book a table in most restaurants, the most expensive of which will take credit cards, but do check first, to avoid embarrassment. Otherwise, pay in roubles and leave a 10 percent tip if service is not included on your bill. Most bars also serve food.

For authentic tea, coffee and cakes, do try the *bulochnayas* (bakeries) on Nevsky Prospekt. Russian tea *(chay)* is served with a slice of lemon and a spoonful of jam, instead of sugar, and the water is boiled in a samovar. Vegetarians should not feel as ostracised as they did in the past. Parents visiting with children will not find restaurants particularly child-friendly.

Gone are the days of cheap eating in St Petersburg, but the city now offers varied menus to cater to all tastes and whims.

Russian Restaurants

Expensive

AKVAREL
Prospekt Dobrulyubova 14a
Tel: 320-8600
Good food, and great views of the embankment; young, fashionable crowd.

OLD CUSTOMS HOUSE
Tamozheny Pereulok 1
Tel: 327-8980
www.concord-catering.ru
Excellent European and Russian cuisine, but pretentious.

SALKHINO
Kronversky Prospekt 25
Tel: 232-7891
Great Georgian cooking, but it doesn't come cheap.

ZOV ILICHA (LENIN'S MATING CALL)
Kazanskaya Ulitsa 34
Tel: 117-8641
The interior is a great parody on the Soviet era, but at capitalist prices. Russian and French cuisine.

Moderate

CAT
Karavannaya Ulitsa 24
Tel: 315-3900
Open noon–11pm.

DEMYANOVA UKHA
Kronversky Prospekt 35 (Petrograd side)
Tel: 232-8090
Open 11am–11pm.
Charming, traditional interior.

NA ZDOROVYE!
Bolshoi Prospekt 13
Tel: 232-4039
Good Russian food served in a folksy, kitschy interior.

NIKOLAI
Bolshaya Morskaya Ulitsa 52
Tel: 311-1402
Open noon–midnight.
Inside the impressive House of the Architect.

RUSSKAYA RIBALKA
Uzhnaya Doroga 11
Tel: 323-9813
The best place for fish, and you can catch your own fish in their pond. It's far from the centre, on Krestovsky Island (on the Petrograd Side)

Russian Cafés

CAFÉ IDIOT
Naberezhnaya Reki Moiki 82
Tel: 315-1675
Opening times vary so check first. It's atmospheric and relaxing, with walls lined with books.

STAROE CAFÉ
Naberezhnaya Reki Fontanki 108
Tel: 316-5111
Open noon–11pm.
With a well-crafted and old-style interior.

International Restaurants

Expensive

DVORIANSKOE GNEZDO (NEST OF THE GENTRY)
Ulitsa Dekabristov 21
Tel: 312-3205

Open 11am–midnight.
Reliably good food

EUROPE RESTAURANT
Mikhailovskaya Ulitsa 1/7
Tel: 329-6000.
Open 7–11pm. Sunday brunch; buffet breakfast Monday–Saturday 7am–10pm.

HERMITAGE
Dvortsovaya Ploshchad 8/6
Tel: 314-4772
The official restaurant of the Hermitage Museum. Great interior, but the mediocre food is overpriced.

KETINO
8th Line 23, Vasilevsky Island
Tel: 326-0196
Serves excellent but quite pricey Georgian cooking. Fine collection of Georgian art on the walls.

MAGRIB
Nevsky Prospekt 84
Tel: 275-1255
Stylish, Middle Eastern interior, but has a reputation for gangster associations

TALEON CLUB (VICTORIA)
Naberezhnaya Reki Moiki 59
Tel: 324-9944
Bar open noon–6am; restaurant open noon–3am. Set inside the sumptuous house of rich 19th-century merchant, Yeliseev.

Moderate
BISTRO LE FRANCAIS
Ulitsa Galernaya 20
Tel: 315-2465
Open 11am–1am. Simple, French cuisine.

CHOPSTICKS
Grand Hotel Europe
Mikhailovskaya Ulitsa 1/7
Tel: 329-6000
Open noon–11pm. Chinese cuisine.

IDIOT
Naberezhnaya Reki Moiki 82
Tel: 315-1675
Great atmosphere, great cappuccino, and good vegetarian meals.

Left: reading room at Cafe Idiot
Above: window at Demyanova Ukha

MACARONI
Rubinstein Ulitsa 23
Tel: 315-6147
This is one of the few fine Italian restaurants in the city.

MAMA ROMA
Karavannaya Ulitsa 3
Tel: 314-0347
Open 11am–2pm. Serves pizzas.

ME 100
Ulitsa Lenin 18 (Petrograd Side)
Tel: 230-5359
Russian, Japanese, and Italian cuisine. Small and stylish restaurant. Great food at what is

probably the most reasonable prices in town. The friendly, English-speaking owner, Katya, is almost always on the premises, ensuring customers are satisfied.

ONEGIN
Sadovaya Ulitsa 11
Tel: 311-8384
Exquisite French and Russian cuisine, but expensive. Exclusive club frequented by local celebrities. DJ late night.

PATIO PIZZA
Nevsky Prospekt 30
Tel: 314-8215
Good pizza, and it's centrally located.

TANDOOR
Voznesensky Prospekt 2
Tel: 312-3886
Open noon–11pm.
Indian cuisine.

TINKOFF
Ulitsa Kazanskaya 7
Tel: 118-5566
Hip club and restaurant. Great salads, pizza and sushi. Has its own micro-brewery.

TROITSKY MOST
Malaya Posadksaya Ulitsa 4
The best bargain in town. Fine and original vegetarian cooking. Hari Khrishna owned.

International Cafés and Bars

CROCODILE
Galernaya Ulitsa 18
Tel: 314-9437
Cult café catering to local bohemian circles. Great food and cool atmosphere.

MARIUS PUB
Ulitsa Marata 11
Tel: 315-4880
Traditional Swiss pub with fine German fare. One of the few places that is open 24 hours

MOLLIE'S IRISH BAR
Ulitsa Rubinshteina 36
Tel: 319-9768
Open 11am–3am.

PROPAGANDA
Naberezhnaya Reki Fontanki 40
Tel: 275-3558
Fashionable café that exploits the Soviet theme, but at more socialistic prices.

SADKO
Grand Hotel Europe,
Ulitsa Mikhailovskaya 1/7
Tel: 329-6000

Open noon–midnight.
A lively bar; cosmopolitan fare.

SSSR
Nevsky Prospekt 54
Tel: 310-4929
Despite the name, there's nothing much Soviet about it. Expensive and fashionable café, that becomes a club late at night.

Coffee Houses

CHE
Poltavskaya Ulitsa 3
Tel: 277-7600
Coolest café in the city, with live jazz daily.

IDEALNAYA CHASKA
Nevsky Prospekt 15, 112 and 130
Tel: 320-6489
Good coffee, at reasonable prices, but not very good desserts. Attracts a young crowd.

MARKO
Nevsky Prospekt 16 and 108
Tel: 275-7559
Good coffee, a variety of salads, and great desserts. It's also a place for students.

MARRAKESH
Karavannaya Ulitsa 3
Tel: 117-8047
Exquisite teahouse for a fashionable crowd.

Internet Cafés

Most Internet cafés are open 24 hours, and are centrally located. Rates are reasonable, a little more than US$2 per hour.

QUO VADIS
Nevsky Prospekt 24
www.quovadis.ru
Hip café; great place to hang out; central.

CAFÉ MAX
Nevsky Prospekt 90
www.cafemax.ru
Popular with young game players.

RED FOG
Kazanskaya Ulitsa 30
www.redfog.net
Best rates; you can check your mail in five minutes for one rouble.

Above: pancakes *(bliny)* and caviar
Right: rock concert Palace Square

NIGHTLIFE

Nightlife in Russia can take many forms and, after the restrictions of the past, there are numerous possibilities. If you visit the city in June, during the White Nights Festival, when it never gets dark, the city hardly sleeps. In winter the fun continues, but it's harder to leave your warm room. A key thing to remember is that you are on a series of islands and you can get marooned – the bridges go up to let ships through in the middle of the night. Before going anywhere very late at night, check bridge times (they vary from 2–5am).

However, most of the organised nightlife ends before you get cut off. Ballet, opera and classical music concerts usually start around 7pm and finish by 9.30pm, giving you plenty of time to move on to the next event. Most theatres take a summer break from mid-July to mid-September. Restaurants close around midnight, although those with built-in discotheques and floor shows stay open much later. Times vary, so check before you go.

Many hotels arrange their own nightlife in bars and discotheques. Visitors with the cash to spare may enjoy a visit to one of the city's casinos.

The club scene is thriving at the moment – young people are hungry for it. Although the increasing accessibility of Western music and culture makes you wonder if you are in Russia, Europe or the US, there are some interesting new and original Russian bands that have emerged from the underground scene that proliferates in abandoned bomb shelters and cinemas. Unfortunately, many clubs do not advertise themselves and venues continually change. Much is still done by word of mouth. Raves are becoming increasingly popular, and the town has incredible venues to accommodate large crowds. There are more organised venues for those who like jazz and rock. English magazines such as *Pulse* and the *St Petersburg Times* will give up-to-date information.

Remember to be careful on the streets. St Petersburg used to be one of the safest cities in Russia; the metro is still regarded as the safest means of transport late at night, but taxis are to be avoided if you are on your own. The metro closes at midnight and reopens at 6am. Buses run until 1am and taxis operate all night.

The city often looks especially beautiful at night – under the snow, or during the White Nights Festival, when late night boat trips can be magical. Check for details through a hotel service bureau for the larger boats, or consult one of the taxi-boat drivers. If you don't feel like clubbing or sitting in a theatre, why not walk, and, making sure you are on the right island, just watch the bridges lift and the boats go through.

The Ballet

The Kirov is now called the Mariinsky Theatre. The ballet enjoys such huge international fame that it is often on tour so you may not see the real thing. But the theatre in itself is spectacular, with a beautiful auditorium, and if you do get seats, it is still considered a privilege. You can book through the tourist offices in any hotel or at the theatre box office, but make sure you do so well in advance. Tickets for foreigners are expensive, but cheaper ones can sometimes be bought on the door.

THE MARIINSKY THEATRE

Teatralnaya Ploshchad 1
Tel: 326-4141
This is where the finest operas and ballets are performed and where dancers such as Pavlova and Nijinsky made their débuts. Former members include Nureyev and Makarova. Seats 1,800.

MUSSORGSKY THEATRE OF OPERA AND BALLET

Ploshchad Iskusstv 1
Tel: 595-4305
Remains open in July and August, when the Mariinsky closes.

Concert Halls

St Petersburg enjoys a rich musical tradition. There are ticket offices at Nevsky Prospekt 42 but the best way to find out what's on is to go to the venues after 11am and ask. Check the companies aren't on tour.

OKTYABRSKY CONCERT HALL

Ligovsky Prospekt 6
Tel: 275-1273
Huge modern building (1967) seating 4,000. Excellent classical and modern performances; also ballets.

THE ST PETERSBURG STATE CAPELLA HALL (GLINKA)

Naberezhnaya Reki Moiki 20
Tel: 314-1058
Glinka and Rimsky Korsakov taught here. Home of the former court choir. Classical and contemporary concerts.

SHOSTAKOVICH ACADEMIC PHILARMONIA

Mikhailovskaya Ulitsa 2
Tel: 110-4257
Originally the Club of the Gentry. Classical concerts staged in the Bolshoi (large) hall. Wagner, among others, conducted here.

For Children

THE BOLSHOI PUPPET THEATRE

Ulitsa Nekrasova 10
Tel: 273-6672
Founded in 1931.

CIRCUS

Naberezhnaya Reki Fontanki 3
Tel: 210-4198
Former home of the Cinizelli Circus. Continues to use performing animals such as bears and monkeys.

Theatres

ALEXANDRINSKY THEATRE (PUSHKIN DRAMA THEATRE)

Ploshchad Ostrovskovo 2
Tel: 110-4103
Beautiful, neo-classical building.

THE BOLSHOI DRAMATIC THEATRE

Naberezhnaya Reki Fontanki 65
Tel: 310-9242
Traditional Russian plays performed here.

MALY DRAMATIC THEATRE

Ulitsa Rubinshteina 18
Tel: 113-2078
Productions at this theatre are more experimental than those at the Bolshoi.

Above: the end of a fine performance

Comic Trust

Underground comedy theatre that uses no language, only music, gestures and mime. This is the 'other' St Petersburg, far from the high culture of the Mariinksy. Check their website for shows: www.comic-trust.com.

Folk Shows

Folk shows feature Russian peasant and Cossack dancers. They are usually excellent.

"Feel Yourself Russian" Show
Nikolayevsky Palace, Ploshchad Truda 4
Tel: 312-5500

Folk Show in Sovietskaya Hotel
Sovietskaya Hotel
Lermontovsky Prospekt 43
Tel: 140-2945

Clubs

The drab and depressing Soviet nights are over and St Petersburg now has a wide range of exciting nightlife. Techno clubs are popular with young people, but there is also a good choice of Russian folk shows. St Petersburg also has a vibrant underground culture, especially cabaret and informal theatres, such as Comic Trust *(see above)*. Most clubs have club-card systems and/or strict on-the-door control, but this is mostly for Russians; foreigners are rarely turned away.

Jakata
Prospekt Bakunin 5
Tel: 346-7461
Two dance floors, and fine cuisine; among the most fashionable clubs.

Onegin
Sadovaya Ulitsa
Tel: 117-8384
Home to the city's most fashionable and beautiful crowd.

Par.Spb
Alexandrovsky Park 5b
Tel: 233-3374
Techno club, popular with foreigners.

Plaza
Naberezhanya Makarov 2
Tel: 323-9090
Upscale and expensive disco, popular with foreigners

Purga
Naberezhanya Reki Fontanki 13
Tel: 313-4123
Very popular; New Year's Eve-style party celebrated every night.

Jet Set
Furshtatskaya Ulitsa 58b
Tel: 275-9288
Door control and club cards. Sumptuous Eastern-style decor; resident European DJs.

Tunnel
In a bunker at the corner of Zverinsky and Lyubanksy Pereulok
Tel: 233-4015
Democratic student club.

Gay Clubs
Greshniki
Naberezhnaya Kanala Griboyedova 29
Tel: 318-4291
Large (male) gay club with medieval theme.

Tri El
5th Sovietskaya Ulitsa, 45
Tel: 110-2016
The city's only lesbian club.

Cabarets
Chaplin Club
Ulitsa Chaikovskogo 59
Tel: 272-6649
City's best comedy club. Some shows are mime, but most are in Russian.

Prival.Com
Corner of Naberezhnaya Reki Moiki and Marsovaya Polye
Tel: 314-3849
Pre-1917 Bohemian hang-out in basement. Good food and fun shows at weekends.

Stray Dog
Ploshchad Isskusstv 5
Tel: 315-7764
Historic club, originally opened in 1912; it was a centre of Silver Age artists. Art exhibits and musical performances, plus dining.

Practical Information

GETTING THERE

When to Visit

The best times to visit St Petersburg are mid-summer and mid-winter. It is hard to be specific about the weather in a city that is so exposed to the elements. There are distinct seasons but there are often freak weather conditions. A strong wind often blows in from the sea, which can be pleasant in the summer.

The long days (White Nights) of summer, from the end of May to the end of July, are a feature of a traditionally romantic time when the atmosphere is festive. The weather can be relatively warm in June, July and August, averaging between 11–21°C (52–70°F). September can be golden and pleasant, averaging 9–15°C (48–59°F).

The city is often less crowded in summer, when people go on holiday and visit their *dachas* (country houses), to tend to their fruit and vegetable gardens. If you want to swim, there are many clear lakes, although the sea water is polluted.

Snow begins to fall in November and by December it settles but quite often melts, to be followed by more snow, creating a horrible slush that is the bane of life in this otherwise wonderful city. This is at its worst in March, a month to avoid. Also try to avoid November, before the snow has really settled. December and January are the coldest months, when temperatures can fall to -17°C (1°F). Spring begins at the end of March.

Visas and Customs

You cannot enter the country without a visa, best arranged through a travel agency. Apply at least three weeks before your visit, or a month in advance if you are travelling independently. Customs declarations forms will be issued on arrival. State how much currency you are bringing into the country and declare valuable items such as jewellery or computer equipment. Don't lose the customs form as it will be needed when you leave, to demonstrate that you are not taking out more money than you brought in. It is unlikely your bags will be searched at customs, but pack them in such a way that it won't be a disaster if they are.

When you leave the country, you must fill out another form and present it with the first. Keep receipts of all goods you have bought during your visit.

Clothing

The most important thing is to be comfortable, so it is essential to have good walking shoes. In the winter your shoes should be waterproof, warm and easy to walk in. There is nothing worse than having cold, wet feet in the snow. Other winter essentials are a very warm coat, a hat (preferably one that covers your ears) and gloves. Buildings are centrally heated, and most have an efficient *Garderob* or cloakroom system, where you can safely leave your belongings. Carry a spare pair of indoor shoes in winter, as you may not want to trudge round a museum or watch the ballet in your boots.

Even if you are travelling in mid-summer, it is a good idea to bring a sweater and jacket, and an umbrella. Sunglasses, suncream, a sunhat and a swimming costume are also recommended.

On the whole, Russians prefer to be smartly dressed, particularly in the evenings and for special occasions, although comfort

Left: Rostral Column
Right: navigating the Cyrillic alphabet

is important, too. Formal dress is obligatory for business meetings.

Useful Items

In summer the mosquitoes can be a real pest, although they do not carry malaria. Take both insect repellent and an anti-mosquito plug-in for your room at night.

Photography

Bring your own film, although there is now a wide selection on offer. There are many Kodak shops that can develop films quickly.

Electricity

Bring a continental adaptor plug for a hairdryer, travelling iron or electric razor, but be aware that some sockets are too narrow for the standard European pins. The standard voltage is 220 volts/50 Hz.

Time Differences

St Petersburg is three hours ahead of British summer time and GMT, two hours ahead of other European cities, and eight hours ahead of New York, so when it is noon in St Petersburg it is 9am in London, 10am in most European capitals and 4am in New York. Summer time, when clocks are put forward by one hour, runs 31 March–30 October.

USEFUL INFORMATION

Specialist Museums

ALEXANDER BLOK APARTMENT MUSEUM

Ulitsa Dekabristov 57
Tel: 113-8627
Open 11am–5pm, closed Wednesday and last Tuesday of every month.

Metro: Sennaya Ploshchad or Sadovaya.
Poet and contemporary of Anna Akhmatova.

ANNA AKHMATOVA MUSEUM

Naberezhnaya Reki Fontanki (Sheremetyev Palace)
Tel: 272-2211
Open 10.30am–5.30pm, closed Monday and last Wednesday of every month.
Metro: Gostinny Dvor.
Museum devoted to the life and work of this famous 20th-century poet.

FYODOR DOSTOEVSKY APARTMENT-MUSEUM

Kuznechny Pereulok 5/2
Tel: 117-4031
Open 11am–6pm, closed Monday.
Metro: Vladimirskaya.
Apartment in which the author died, having written *The Brothers Karamazov*.

APARTMENT-MUSEUM OF THE ELIZAROVS

Ulitsa Lenina 52, Apartment 24
Tel: 235-3778
Open 10am–6pm, closed Wednesday and Sunday. Metro: Petrogradskaya.
Apartment belonging to Lenin's sister, where he sometimes stayed.

PUSHKIN APARTMENT-MUSEUM

Naberezhnaya Reki Moyki 12
Tel: 117-3531
Open 11am–5pm, closed Tuesday.
Metro: Gostinny Dvor.
Overlooking the River Moyka. Pushkin, Russia's greatest poet, lived and worked here for a year before his fatal duel with a Frenchman in 1837.

MEMORIAL MUSEUM OF LENINGRAD DEFENCE AND THE SIEGE
Solyanoy Pereulok 9
Tel: 275-7208
Open 10am–5pm, closed Wednesday and last Thursday of every month.
Metro: Chernyshevskaya.

MILITARY-HISTORICAL MUSEUM OF ARTILLERY, ENGINEERS AND SIGNAL CORPS
Alexandrovsky Park 7
Tel: 232-0296
Open 11am–5pm, closed Monday, Tuesday and last Thursday of every month.
Metro: Gorkovskaya.

MUSEUM OF THE HISTORY OF ST PETERSBURG
Peter and Paul Fortress
Tel: 238-0511
Open 11am–5pm, closed Wednesday. Additional branch: The Ryumantsev Mansion, *Angliiskaya Naberezhnaya 44, tel: 117-7544.*

THEATRE AND MUSIC MUSEUM
Ploshchad Ostrovskogo 6
Tel: 117-2195
Open 11am–6pm; Wednesday 1–7pm closed Tuesday.

Left: bathing beside the fortress
Above: Yusupov's Palace

YUSUPOV PALACE
Naberezhnaya Reki Moiki 94
Tel: 314-9883
Open daily, telephone in advance to check times. Metro: Sennaya Ploshchad.
This is where Rasputin was murdered.

RELIGION

Religion, declared 'the opium of the people' by Karl Marx, is now playing an increasingly important role in people's lives. Since Gorbachev's time, many churches have been reopened for worship. Most Russian Orthodox churches have a morning Divine Liturgy at 10am and an evening service at 6pm. Women are required to cover their heads in churches; and long skirts or trousers should be worn to avoid causing offence. If you wish to take photographs, you should ask a member of staff first.

Russian Orthodox

HOLY TRINITY CATHEDRAL, ALEXANDER-NEVSKY LAVRA
Naberezhnaya Monastryrku Reki 1
Tel: 274-0409
Metro: Ploshchad Alexandra Nevskovo.

KAZAN CATHEDRAL
Kazansky Ploshchad 2 (actual address, but it's on Nevsky Prospekt)
Tel: 318-4528
Seat of the St Petersburg Metropolitan, Orthodoxy's local cathedral. Tours daily.

SPASSO-PREOBRAZHENSKY (OUR SAVIOUR TRANSFIGURATION) CATHEDRAL
Preobrazhenskaya Ploshchad 1
Tel: 272-3662
Metro: Chernyshevskaya.

ST NICHOLAS (SAILORS') CATHEDRAL
Nikolskaya Ploshchad 1/3
Tel: 114-6926
Metro: Sennaya Ploshchad or Sadovaya.

CHURCH OF OUR SAVIOUR ON SPILLED BLOOD (KHRAM SPAS-NA-KROVI)
Konyushennaya Ploshchad
Tel: 315-1636
Metro: Nevsky Prospekt.00

Other

THE ROMAN CATHOLIC CHURCH OF
OUR LADY OF LOURDES
Kovensky Pereulok 7
Tel: 272-0442
Metro: Ploshchad Vosstaniya

ST CATHERINE'S OF ALEXANDRIA
ROMAN CATHOLIC CHURCH
Nevsky Prospekt 32–34
Tel: 117-5795
Daily services; in English Sunday 9.30am.

THE BUDDHIST TEMPLE
Primorsky Prospekt 91
Tel: 430-0341
Metro: Staraya Derevnya.

THE ST PETERSBURG
CONGREGATIONAL MOSQUE
Kronversky Prospekt 7
Tel: 233-9819
Metro: Gorkovskaya.

EVANGELICAL LUTHERAN CHURCH
OF ST PETER
Nevsky Prospekt 22/24
Tel: 311-2423
Metro: Nevsky Prospekt or Gostinny Dvor.

THE ST PETERSBURG GREAT
CHOIR SYNAGOGUE
Lermontovsky Prospekt 2
Tel: 114-0078
Metro: Sennaya Ploshchad or Sadovaya.

MONEY MATTERS

Currency

You will need roubles. There is now a wide range of banking services, including ATM machines. Always present your passport when changing money. It is illegal to import or export roubles. You may bring in as much hard currency as you want if it is declared *(see page 75)*.

Safety

Strange as it may sound, foreigners are more likely to be victimised by the police *(militsiya)* than by street thugs. The Russian police are notoriously corrupt, and have ties to criminal groups. Social surveys consistently show that the Russian people do not trust them. President Putin is waging a campaign to clean up the *militsiya*, but so far it appears in vain. Attacks most often happen late at night. The police usually wait near night-clubs and bars, and prey on those coming out, especially those who are more than a little tipsy. Russian law requires you to carry your passport, and if police catch you without one, they have the right to detain you for several days. My only advice is, avoid the police after dark. If cornered, insist that you want to call your consulate.

Credit Cards

Western restaurants and hotels usually accept major bank cards and travellers' cheques but be sure to confirm when you book. Hard currency can be drawn from your account with a bank card.

Tipping

As in most European countries, an average tip is about 10 percent. Tip in roubles. If you have agreed a fare with a taxi driver there is no need to tip.

GETTING AROUND

Geography

St Petersburg, Russia's largest seaport and second-largest city, lies on a parallel 60° north of the equator – the same latitude as Alaska and Oslo. Finland is 160 km (99 miles) to the north. The city straddles 101 islands at the mouth of the great River Neva,

which sweeps majestically through its centre, emptying Lake Ladoga 74 km (45 miles) to the east into the Gulf of Finland to the west. Granite embankments contain the 65 rivers, canals, channels and streams which separate all the islands but flooding occurs when gales come in from the Baltic.

There are 365 bridges joining the islands. These waterways, Lake Ladoga and the sea all freeze over in winter but icebreakers keep the port open throughout the year.

From the Admiralty on the south embankment, the main streets radiate as spokes of a wheel; the canals and other streets cross these spokes running parallel to the main channel of the Neva.

The streets have nearly all reverted to their pre-revolutionary names and it is no longer necessary to know the Soviet versions. Russian addresses are given in reverse order, with street names followed by house or apartment number.

Below are a few essential terms that will come in useful for finding your way around:

Ulitsa – street
Ploshchad – square
Pereulok – small street
Naberezhnaya – embankment
Most – bridge
Ostrov – island
Prospekt – prospect
Linia – line

Left: in the Church of the Anunication
Above: the Pushkin metro station

Taxis

Official taxis are yellow with a 'T' sign and a chequered light or strip on the side. Taxi ranks have long since gone out of use and taxis that congregate outside hotels will always demand a higher price. It is cheaper to stick your arm out on the street, but you should always bargain. Newer yellow cabs are fitted with a meter but agree a fee with drivers of the older cabs. The private cabs that compete with the yellow taxis also charge a flat fee. It will be easier if you learn a few Russian numbers so that you can establish a price with the driver before you set off – or take a notepad and write the figure out.

Most locals aim to catch a *chastnik* – a private vehicle flagged down, rather than a taxi, but this is not recommended for visitors to the city.

DVUCH STOLITS
Tel: 928-0000
City centre to airport, 600 roubles.

SEVERNAYA PALMIRA
Tel: 312-6300
City centre to airport, 450 roubles.

TAXI BLUES
Tel: 271-8888
City centre to airport, 450 roubles.

practical information

Metro

The metro runs from about 6am to midnight. It is fast, cheap, clean and famous for its architecture and design. It is well worth mastering, although it can seem daunting at first if you don't understand the cyrillic alphabet. If in doubt, avoid journeys where you have to change to another line. Metro stations are marked above ground with an 'M' sign. You buy your *zheton* or token at the kiosk, then feed it into the barrier; a green light comes on and you walk through onto a fast-moving escalator; keep to the right-hand side.

The Electric Railway

Many locals use this service to take them to their *dachas*. Local trains run from the Finland, Vitebsk, and Baltic stations, all of which are served by their own metros. It is the cheapest way to travel out to one of the palaces. A ticket system operates here, so make sure you buy a return.

Buses and Trolleybuses

These run from 6am to 1am. If you decide to make full use of this system, try to acquire a map called 'Marshruti Gorodskovo Transporta – Trolleibus, Avtobus i Trambai': Town transport routes for Trolleybuses, Buses and Trams. Without one, you could easily get lost. Sometimes they are easy to purchase, but at other times they fall out of circulation. Ask at a hotel service bureau or visit the Ost-West Kontaktservice *(see page 90)*.

During the rush hour the buses and trolleybuses are extremely crowded. Look for an 'A' sign to signify a bus stop and a 'T' for a Trolleybus. Tickets are bought from the conductor.

Car Hire
Hertz
Malaya Morskaya Ulitsa 23
Tel: 324-3242
www.hertz.spb.ru

Boats

Regular boat trips with a Russian guide on large, covered boats leave from Dvortsovaya Naberezhnaya, in front of the Hermitage, and take you along four of the river embankments. Each trip lasts approximately one hour. There is also a covered boat excursion of the same duration that explores the rivers and canals from the Anichkov Bridge on the Nevsky Prospekt. Taxi-boats – smaller, open-topped boats that seat up to 10 people, can usually be found on Narodny Bridge as the Nevsky crosses the Moika Canal. Hydrofoil boats to Petrodvoretz also leave from outside the Hermitage, from a different pier. Boats do not operate in winter or when it is windy.

Bridges

From April to early November the bridges *(most)* open up in the early hours of the morning, some of them twice, to let ships through. Usual times range between 1.55 and 4.50am. One thing you don't want is to become stranded on the wrong island.

HOURS AND HOLIDAYS
Business Hours

Don't expect places to be open when they say they will. The sign *Na Remont* – under restoration – is an all too familiar one. Everywhere has its own opening and closing times,

practical information

so it is best to check times individually. In general, most department stores are open between 10am–7pm.

Make sure you get to museums at least one hour before their official closing times or you will be refused admittance.

Check restaurant times individually on the day. Private cafés are not always predictable and generally close for an hour after they have served lunch and before they reopen for dinner.

Food markets open between 8am–7pm, but close at 4pm on Sunday.

Public Holidays

Some of the main holidays are as follows:

1–2 January – **New Year Holiday**
7 January – **Orthodox Christmas**
March/April (dates vary) – **Orthodox Easter**
21 June–11 July – **White Nights Festival**
12 December – **Day of the Constitution of Russia**

ACCOMMODATION

Unless staying with friends, or renting an apartment, accommodation is usually arranged automatically through your tour operator or travel agent. However, it is worth knowing a little about the hotel situation so you know what to expect.

For most of the 1990s, visitors only had about five decent hotels to choose from. The city's 300th anniversary, however, stimulated a boom in hotel construction, especially small guesthouses and B&Bs.

After its recent restoration, the Astoria Hotel, owned and managed by Sir Rocco Forte, is now up to par with the city's leading hotel, the Grand Hotel Europe. Have a coffee in the Astoria's lobby café and enjoy the magnificent view of St Isaac's Square. The Angleterre, also owned by Sir Rocco Forte, and the Hotel Dostoevsky, make for a good choice in the three-star range. For something clean and pleasant, but with an eye on budget, the best bet is the US-owned and operated Rand House, and its neighbouring competitor, Comfort Hotel. A cheaper option is a youth hostel or campsite. A small selection of hotels follows.

Left: commuter train
Above: Grand Hotel Europe

Hotels
Five star
Standard rooms from US$260 a night

ASTORIA HOTEL
Bolshaya Morskaya Ulitsa 39
Tel: 313-5757; fax: 313-5134
E-mail: reserve@astoria.spb.ru
www.roccofortehotels.com
The Astoria opened its doors in December 1912, and after the Bolsheviks seized power, a number of revolutionaries live here. The rooms are recently refurbished, but service sometimes seems stuck in the Soviet era. It is centrally located on St. Isaac's Square, and most tourist sites can be reached on foot. Two died here in a gangland killing a few years ago, so don't be surprised if you see unsavoury types in the lobby. The Davidov restaurant offers fine dining.

GRAND HOTEL EUROPE
Mikhailovskaya Ulitsa 7
Tel: 329-6000; fax: 329-6001
E-mail: hotel@ghe.spb.ru
www.grandhoteleurope.com
Commonly referred to as the Europa by locals, this was Russia's first five-star hotel in the post-Soviet period, and continues to attract the city's most elite travellers, which have included Bill Clinton and Paul McCartney. The rooms are spacious and decorated with period furniture. The hotel offers the finest dining opportunities in the city, with seven restaurants, including Chinese, Italian, European and Russian cuisines.

RADISSON SAS ROYAL HOTEL
Nevsky Prospekt 49
Tel: 322-5000; fax: 322-5002
E-mail: stpetersburg@radissonsas.com
www.radissonsas.com
The rooms tend to be small and the lobby is not impressive, so many consider this hotel falls way behind its competitors in the luxury range. The 18th-century building was entirely gutted and renovated several years ago, so today it provides a complete range of modern services. Its first-floor Cannelle bar and café is one of the best places in the city to get a drink and watch life pass by on one of the busiest intersections.

CORINTHIA NEVSKIJ PALACE HOTEL
Nevsky Prospekt 57
Tel: 380-2001; fax: 380-1937
E-mail: reservation@corinthia.ru
www.corinthia.ru
Commonly called the Nevsky Palace, it is the preferred accommodation for upscale business travellers, and it does an excellent job of providing conference services. Located near the far end of Nevsky Prospekt, it means you will need to walk further to major tourist sites or have to take a car. There's a wonderful Sunday brunch at the Imperial restaurant, while the rooftop Landskrona is ranked one of the best places to eat in the city, and has a wonderful view.

Four star
Standard rooms from US$200 a night

ANGLETERRE HOTEL
Bolshaya Morskaya Ulitsa 39
Tel: 313-5666; fax: 313-5125
E-mail: reservation@angleterrehotel.spb.ru
www.angleterrehotel.com
The Angleterre is part of the Sir Rocco Forte empire, but unlike the Astoria it caters to the budget-conscious traveller who still expects fine service. The hotel has excellent business services, and a fitness centre and pool, as well as a casino and nightclub on the first floor. Since it has the same fine location on St Isaac's Square as the Astoria, many travellers have come to realise the Anglettere is better value for money.

BALTIC STAR HOTEL
Beriozovaya Alley 3, Strelna
Tel: 438-5700; fax: 438-5888
E-mail: info@balticstarhotel.ru
The Baltic Star is the best option for travellers who prefer to get away from the noise and pollution of the busy town centre. It is located on the Gulf of Finland, in the grounds of the magnificent park of the recently renovated Konstantin Palace, which is an official residence of the Russian government. The rooms tend to be small, but the service is excellent. Also available are 20 high-security cottages that comfortably sleep up to 10 people. The city centre is about a 45-minute drive.

GRAND HOTEL EMERALD
Suvorovsky Prospekt 18
Tel: 140-5000; fax: 114-5001
E-mail: info@grandhotelemerald.com
www.grandhotelemerald.com
This is one of St Petersburg's most modern hotels, and it is working hard to prove itself worthy on the market. Rooms are large and comfortable. The sleek, steel modern exterior contrasts with a more distinguished Classical interior, which leaves you feeling as if you're staying in a tsarist palace. It has a health spa that includes a Russian bath and a Turkish sauna. While it is close to the city hall, you need to drive to the main tourist destinations.

practical information

ALEXANDER HOUSE

Naberezhnaya Krukov Canal 27
Tel: (812) 259-6877
E-mail: info@a-house.ru
www.a-house.ru
Alexander House provides some of the city's best luxury VIP apartments, but at three-star prices. Close to the Mariinsky Theatre, it is better suited to those on long stays. Rooms are spacious with high ceilings, and the interior of each is individually decorated according to a major international style. Three people can easily fit in each apartment, and there is a bridal suite.

KAZANSKY HOTEL

Ulitsa Kazanskaya 5
Tel: 327-7466 and 327-7467
www.kazansky5.com
This small, exquisite, upscale hotel is in the very heart of the city, just behind the Kazan Cathedral. Partially furnished with genuine antique furniture, it recreates the gentile atmosphere of old St Petersburg. Family-run, the hotel gives the impression that you've been invited into a home. A minor snag is that the entrance is on the third floor, and there is no lift.

Three Star

Standard rooms from US$80 a night.

PRIBALTIISKAYA HOTEL

Ulitsa Korablestroiteley,14
Tel: 356-3001 and 356-2157; fax: 356-6094
E-mail: market@pribaltiyskaya.ru
www.pribaltiyskaya.ru
The name literally means 'by the Baltic', and nothing could be truer. Located on land's end on the Gulf of Finland, the hotel offers an impressive view of the sea. It is one of the largest hotels in the city, and is the perfect place for large groups, but you will need to arrange bus transport, as the city centre is a 20-minute journey, if there's no traffic, and up to a 45-minute one if there is. Most rooms are still Soviet style in decor, but they are comfortable.

PULKOVSKAYA HOTEL

Ploshchad Pobedy 1
Tel: 140-3900/140-4311
E-mail: info@pulkovskaya.spb.ru

www.pulkovskaya.spb.ru
Conveniently located about 10 minutes' from the city airport on one of the main thoroughfares, this hotel provides easy access to the city centre. You can take the metro – the stop is a short walk away. The hotel certainly has a Soviet feel to it, but rooms are comfortable. There is a congress hall that seats 600 people, as well as a pleasant Bavarian restaurant.

HOTEL MOSKVA

Ploshchad Alexandra Nevskogo 2
Tel: 274-0022 and 274-2052;
fax: 274-2130
E-mail: business@hotel-moscow.ru
www.hotel-moscow.ru
Located just across from the picturesque domes and spires of the Alexander Nevsky Lavra, this Soviet-era hotel stands in stark contrast. It is located at the very end of Nevsky Prospekt, and on one side flows the Neva River. Rooms vary, with some modern and comfortable, while others still retain their Soviet style. This hotel is more popular with large groups.

BEST WESTERN NEPTUNE HOTEL

Naberezhnaya Obvodnogo Kanala 93a
Tel: 324-4610; fax: 324-4611
Email: hotel@neptun.spb.ru
www.neptun.spb.ru
While it is located in one of the worst places in the city centre – along the dismal, industrial Obvodny Canal, which is very slowly being modernized – the hotel provides a host of services for the business traveller, among which are three conference halls. It also has one of the city's best fitness centres and swimming pools, as well as an eight-lane bowling alley.

Left: conference facilities serve the city's growing business sector
Above: perspective on Peter the Great's coat of arms

OKTYABRYSKY HOTEL
Ligovsky Prospekt 10
Tel: 277-6330; fax: 315-7501
E-mail: hotel@oktober.spb.ru
www.oktober-hotel.spb.ru
Built in the mid-19th century, this hotel still retains the charm of a bygone era with its large windows and high ceilings. While it was considered a luxury hotel in tsarist times, today it is regarded as comfortable but not upscale. Its location on Vosstaniya Ploschad (square) across from the Moscow Station makes it easy to reach for those arriving by train from Moscow.

HOTEL ST PETERSBURG
Pirogovskaya Naberezhnaya 5
Tel: 380-1919; fax: 380-1920
E-mail: reservation@hotel-spb.ru
www.hotel-spb.ru
While this dreary Soviet structure is the city centre's worst eyesore, it has one of the best views of the Neva River and the *Avrora* battleship. It offers both modernised and non-modernised rooms, but service leaves much to be desired. Its location, across the river from the centre, makes getting around difficult, and you are dependent on the expensive hotel taxis or your own hire car.

HOTEL DOSTOEVSKY
Vladimirsky Prospekt 19
Tel: 331-3200; fax: 331-3201
E-mail: info@dostoevsky-hotel.ru
www.dostoevsky-hotel.ru
The city's newest hotel offers a great view of one of the most beautiful churches, the St Vladimir Cathedral. The hotel only occupies the top three floors of the building, while down below there is a shopping arcade with fine restaurants and cafés. There are four conference halls, a fitness club and sauna, as well as a nightclub in the hotel.

HELVETIA HOTEL SUITES
Ulitsa Marata 11
Tel: 117-9597; fax: 110-6546
Email: info@helvetia-suites.ru
www.helvetia-suites.ru
This quiet and private apartment hotel is located in a courtyard just next to the Swiss Embassy, so you can be sure security is quite high. Apartments are finely decorated and serviced, and overall it is considered one of the best bargains in town. The neighbouring area also has good restaurants, and Nevsky Prospekt is a short walk away.

MATISOV DOMIK
Naberezhnaya Reki Pryazhky 3
Tel: 318-7051 and 318-5445; fax: 318-7419
Email: matisov@lek.ru
www.matisov.spb.ru
This is one of St Petersburg's first budget hotels, opened in 1993, and is experienced in receiving guests. It offers modern, clean and airy rooms, some of which have a view of the canal. Its location on a small island at the edge of the city's historic centre means you need a car to get to the central sites, although the Mariinsky Theatre is about a 15-minute walk away.

practical information

NAUTILUS INN

Ulitsa Rizhskaya 3
Tel: 449-9000; fax: 449-9009
Email: info@nautilus-inn.ru
www.nautilus-inn.ru
This hotel, just across the Neva River from the Alexander Nevsky Lavra, offers bright and clean rooms. It caters to business travellers and provides the appropriate services, including conference and work facilities. The centre is about a 20-minute journey if the traffic is not heavy.

ARBAT NORD HOTEL

Artilleriiskaya Ulitsa 4
Tel: 103-1899; fax: 103-1898
Email: info@arbat-nord.ru
www.arbat-nord.ru
Located in a district that is home to many foreign consulates, this hotel offers fine modern accommodation at a reasonable price. Staff are very attentive, and there is a nice restaurant on the ground floor. Rooms offer wireless Internet access and satellite TV. The Summer Gardens are a short walk away, while Nevsky Prospekt is not much further.

HOTEL OKHTINSKAYA

Bolsheokhtinsky Prospekt 4
Tel: 222-8601; fax: 227-2514
Email: info@okhtinskaya.spb.ru
www.okhtinskaya.spb.ru
This hotel's location, across the Neva River from the Smolny Cathedral, gives some of the rooms a breathtaking view, but also means it's not easy to get to the centre if you don't have a car and don't wish to be held hostage to the taxi drivers who prey on hotel visitors. However, the hotel offers free hourly shuttles to Nevsky Prospekt. The rooms are comfortable and clean, and the staff are quite helpful.

RUSS

Artilleriiskaya Ulitsa 1
Tel: 273-4683; fax: 279-3600
adminruss@comset.ru
www.hotelruss.spb.ru
The architecture of this Soviet-era hotel clashes with the surrounding 19th-century facades, but the rooms are decent. Service, however, leaves much to be desired. Most travellers tend to be businessmen from elsewhere in Russia and other republics of the former Soviet Union.

B&B/Mini-hotels

Standard rooms from US$40 a night

RAND HOUSE *(www.randhouse.ru)*

Bolshaya Morskaya Ulitsa 25, Flat 17 (3rd floor), tel: 314-6333
Grivtsova Lane 11, Flat 83 (4th floor), tel: 310-7005
Admiralteyskaya Embankment 6, Flats 19 and 20, tel: 312-7152
Sadovaya Street 11, Flat 50 (3rd floor), tel: 315-1037
US-owned and managed, this chain of B&B establishments offers comfortable and modern rooms in historic city-centre buildings. The Grivtsova Lane location is more for budget travellers, while the Admiralteyskaya Embankment provides the high standard preferred by well-heeled travellers.

COMFORT HOTEL

Bolshaya Morskaya Ulitsa 25
Tel: 314-6523; fax: 318-6700
E-mail: info@comfort-hotel.ru
www.comfort-hotel.spb.ru
This mini-hotel's location in the very heart of the city, on a street that runs between Nevsky Prospekt and St Isaac's Square, makes it a prized place to stay. Rooms are well furnished and comfortable.

Left: Hotel St Petersburg
Above: at times, Matrioshka dolls seem to be all around you

PUSHKA INN
Naberezhnaya Reki Moika 14
Tel: 312-0913; fax: 117-9557
E-mail: pushka@pushkainn.ru
www.pushkainn.ru
In an 18th-century building on one of the most picturesque bends in the Moika Canal, a stone's throw from the Hermitage and Palace Square. Rooms are elegant and do justice to the enchantment of old St Petersburg. On the ground floor is one of the city's popular watering holes, the Pushka Inn.

KORONA GUEST CENTRE
Malaya Konnyushennaya Ulitsa 7
Tel: 117-0086; fax: 314-3865
E-mail: korona-spb@peterlink.ru
www.korona-spb.com
This hotel's main advantage is its location on one of the city centre's few pedestrianised streets, and a quiet one at that. Rooms are nicely furnished and the hotel offers a range of services usually reserved for upscale hotels, such as satellite TV, heated floors, safe, Internet access, and free tea round the clock.

AUSTRIAN YARD
Furshtatskaya Ulitsa 45
Tel/fax: 279-8235
Email: natali@austrianyard.com
www.austrianyard.com
The hotel is next to the Austrian embassy and provides high security. Rooms live up to the Austrian reputation for efficiency and cleanliness, and guests can use a sauna and play billiards. One of the city centre's few parks, Tavride Park, is just down the block.

Above: amateur portraits are big business
Right: a moment of tranquillity

THE FIVE CORNERS HOTEL
Zagorodny Prospekt 13
Tel/fax: 380-8181
Email: booking@5ugol.com
www.5ugol.ru
This mini-hotel is located on the second and third floors of one of the city centre's most famous landmark intersections. The rooms are well designed, comfortable and clean. The staff are very helpful, and offer small amenities, such as hot drinks and sandwiches, 24 hours a day. The entrance is next door to an electronics store on Zagorodny Prospekt.

PRESTIGE HOTEL
Third Line 52, Vasilevsky Island
Tel: 328-5338; fax: 328-4228
Email: reservations@prestige-hotels.com
www.prestige-hotels.com
For something central but away from the usual hustle and bustle, try this hotel, located in the historic section of Vasilevsky Island, which is just a short ride from the Hermitage. Rooms are basic, but clean and modern, and some even offer Jacuzzis.

MARSHAL HOTEL
Shpalernaya Ulitsa 41
Tel: 279-9955
Email: marshal.hotel@tpark.spb.ru
www.marshal-hotel.spb.ru
Close to the Tavride Park and to the Smolny Cathedral, this hotel is located in a building dating from 1806 that was once the headquarters for one of the Tsar's cavalry regiments. Rooms are basic and clean and offer Internet access. There are also three conference rooms and a sauna in the hotel.

Youth Hostels

ST PETERSBURG INTERNATIONAL YOUTH HOSTEL
3rd Sovietskaya Ulitsa 28
Tel: 329-8018; fax: 329-8019
E-mail: ryh@rh.ru
www.ryh.ru
Located in a historic working-class neighbourhood not far from the Moscow railway station, this US-owned hostel offers accommodation in single-sex dormitories in a 19th-century building. Rooms are basic but clean.

SLEEP CHEAP
Ul. Mokhovaya 18/32
Tel: 273-5709; fax: 115-1304
Email: hostel@sleepcheap.spb.ru
www.sleepcheap.spb.ru
This is the best bargain for the budget traveller. Located in the heart of the historic centre near the Fontanka River and the Summer Gardens, it offers clean and recently renovated dorms. A small breakfast is included.

INTERNATIONAL HOSTEL HOLIDAY
Ulitsa Mikhailova 1
Tel: 327-1070; fax: 327-1033
E-mail: info@hostel.spb.ru
www.hostel.ru

Campsites

RETUR MOTEL-CAMPING
Bolshaya Kupalnaya Ulitsa, 28
Town of Sestroretsk
Tel: 437-7533
www.retur.ru

HEALTH AND EMERGENCIES

It is advisable to take medicines with you, although chemists do sell foreign medicines and you can find most things you need.

The most common ailment is mild stomach upset, but there is a more serious complaint that can be picked up from drinking contaminated water containing the parasite *Giardia lamblia*. Avoid drinking unboiled water at all costs. Ideally, water should boil for 10 minutes. Purification tablets are no use and unboiled water is often used to make ice, even in the best hotels. Beware of salads that look watery. But don't be too alarmed by the 'Leningrad water disease'. It won't kill you, although it will cause severe diarrhoea, the cure for which is antibiotics. Ask your own doctor what you should take with you as the recommended treatment.

Avoid drinking alcohol bought from street kiosks. Remember that it is important to have medical insurance.

Health Clinics

There's no reason to fear medical treatment in Russia. There are a number of fine Western clinics with the most modern medicine and the best Russian doctors, well versed in both Western and Eastern medical traditions. Rates are not cheap, but lower than you might find at market rates in the West.

AMERICAN MEDICAL CLINIC
Nagerezhnaya Reki Moiki 78
Tel: 140-2090
www.amclinic.com
English-speaking doctors; open 24 hours.

BRITISH-AMERICAN FAMILY PRACTICE
Grafsky Pereulok 7
Tel: 327-6030
www.british-americanclinic.com
Full-time British GP on hand, and English-speaking Russian doctors; open 24 hours.

INTERNATIONAL CLINIC
Ulitsa Dostoyevkovo 19
Tel: 320-3870
www.icspb.com
English-speaking Russian doctors.

DENTAL SERVICES, MEDI
Nevsky Prospekt 82
Tel: 324-0000
www.emedi.ru
The city's best dental clinic. Open 24 hours.

Emergency Numbers

(Free of charge)
Fire 01
Police 02
Ambulance 03
Special Police (for foreigners) 164-9787

Crime

St Petersburg used to be one of the safest cities in the world; this is no longer the case, though it is not as dangerous as people say. In general, the laws of common sense apply. If something is stolen, report the theft to the police immediately and ensure that they issue you with a certificate showing the precise date and time. Little may be done to retrieve your property but you can claim on your insurance. If you are travelling with a group, try to obtain a certificate from your tour operator or guide as well. There is a **Lost and Found Office** at Zakharevskaya 19, tel: 278-3690 (open Monday–Friday 11am–5.30pm).

Russian Baths

The Russian bath is one of the country's most revered institutions, and a place of male bonding. Russian men often like to get their clothes off, get into a hot steam bath, drink vodka, and sometimes invite some 'girls' in – quite often those available for hire. Incidentally, don't be shocked by the prevalence, and acceptance, of prostitution in Russia.

IMBIR

5th Line, Vasilevsky Island
Tel: 323-4275
Newly renovated, with common bath and sauna; Russian billiards also on hand. Rates: VIP section costs US$10 for two hours.

Above: theatre schedule
Right: furry hats for frigid nights

SMOLENSK BATHS

Ulitsa Krasnovo Tektilshika 7
Tel: 110-0969
There's a common bath, and a VIP room for private groups. Best to order this in advance. Rates: US$10–$30 for 1½ hours.

Public Toilets

Prepare yourself for the worst: the standard of many public toilets is utterly disgusting. There will not always be loo paper, so take your own. But toilets in cafés and restaurants are often clean and pleasant.

COMMUNICATIONS

Digital technology has brought St Petersburg into the modern age and enables the city to enjoy direct dialling, leaving the archaic phone system of the Soviet era buried in the past. **Telephone Information Service** (private numbers excluded), tel: 09.
City Information Line (English and Russian), tel: 326-9696.
Long-distance and international calls can be made using credit cards. St Petersburg pay phones inside green booths take phonecards, which can be purchased at metro stations and newsstands.

Postage

CENTRAL POST OFFICE

Ulitsa Pochtantskaya 9
Tel: 312-8302
Metro: Nevsky Prospekt
Open Monday–Saturday 9am–7.30pm, Sunday 10am–5.30pm.

Express mail can be sent via:
DHL, tel: 326-6400
TNT, tel: 118-3330.

International Telephone Calls

For calls outside Russia, dial 8, await the dialling tone, then dial 10 followed by the country code. For US visitors, international access codes are: World Phone 346-8022; AT&T 325-5042.

Media

The past decade has seen an explosion in the number of Russian newspapers and magazines being produced. The Friday edition of *The St Petersburg Times* (www.sptimesrussia.com) and *Pulse* (www. pulse.ru), both published in English, supply up-to-the-minute listings of events and city news. *The Travellers' Yellow Pages* to St Petersburg also provides a wealth of information. These should all be available from hotels in the city. *Northern Cartographic/Russian Information Services* produce up-to-date maps of the city.

Radio and Television

If you bring a multi-band radio you will be able to pick up many English-language broadcasts including the BBC World Service (SW) and Voice of America (SW).

TOUR OPERATORS

If you want to explore beyond St Petersburg, tickets for travel by rail or air, to any city in Russia and the Commonwealth of Independent States, can be purchased at any travel agency. There are plenty to choose from; among them are:

LENART TOURS
Nevsky Prospekt 40
Tel: 312-6553
www.lenart.spb.su

WILD RUSSIA
Naberezhnaya Reki Fontanki 58
Tel: 313-8030
www.wildrussia.spb.ru
Specialises in tourism to Russia's wilderness areas.

ECLECTICA GUIDE
Nevsky Prospekt 44
Tel: 110-5579
gid@eclectica.spb.ru
Specialises in tours of St Petersburg and its suburbs.

EMBASSIES AND CONSULATES

AUSTRALIA
Italyanskaya Ulitsa 1
Tel: 325-7333
www.australianembassy.ru

CANADA
Malodet-skoselsky Prospekt 32
Tel: 325-8448

CHINA
Naberezhnaya Kanala Griboedeva 134
Tel: 114-7670

FINLAND
Ulitsa Chaikovskovo 71
Tel: 273-7321

FRANCE
Naberezhnaya Reki Moiki 15
Tel: 314-1443

GERMANY
Furshtadskaya 39
Tel: 320-2400
www.germanconsulate.spb.ru

INDIA
Ulitsa Rileyeva 35
Tel: 272-1988
www.indianembassy.ru

ISRAEL
Inzhenernaya Ulitsa 6
Tel: 272-0456

SWEDEN
Malaya Konyushennaya Ulitsa 1/3

Tel: 329-1430
www.sweden.spb.ru

UNITED KINGDOM
Ploshchad Proletarskoi Dictatury 5
Tel: 320-3200
www.britain.spb.ru

USA
Ulitsa Furshtadskaya 15
Tel: 331-2600
www.stpetersburg-usconsulate.ru

LANGUAGE

It will help you enormously, particularly when using the metro and reading maps, to have an understanding of the Cyrillic alphabet. Don't be daunted by it – once you have learnt it, you won't forget it.

To transliterate some Russian letters, English letter combinations are used:
Ω = zh, x = kh, c = ts, , = sh, w = shch, ü = yu, ä = ya, ö = yo.

The Russian letter combination ks is transliterated both as ks and as x. Russian letters are transliterated (with a few exceptions) in a similar way: j, y = y, e, ö = e.

The first two columns printed below show the printed letter in Russian upper and then lower case. The third column shows how the Russian letters sound and the fourth column shows the transliteration into English.

1	2	3	4
A	a	a, archaeology	a
B	b	b, buddy	be
V	v	v, vow	v
G	g	g, glad	ge
D	d	d, dot (the tip of the tongue close to the teeth)	de
E	e	e, get	ye
Ö	ö	yo, yoke	
˘	Ω	zh, composure	zhe
Z	z	z, zest	ze
I	i	i, ink	i
J	j	j, yes	jot
K	k	k, kind	ka
L	l	l, life (but a bit harder)	el'
M	m	m, memory	em
N	n	n, nut	en
O	o	o, optimum	o
P	p	p, party	pe
R	r	r (rumbling – as in Italian, the tip of the tongue is vibrating)	er
S	s	s, sound	es
T	t	t, title (the tip of the tongue close to the teeth)	te
U	u	u, nook	u
F	f	f, flower	ef
X	x	kh, hawk	ha
C	c	ts, (pronounced conjointly)	tse
Ç	ç	ch, charter	che
Í	,	sh, shy	sha
W	w	shch, (pronounced conjointly) shcha	
`		(the hard sign)	
Y	y	y (pronounced with the same position of a tongue as when pronouncing G, K)	y
´		(the soft sign)	
Q	q	e, ensign	e
Ü	ü	yu, you	yu
Ä	ä	ya, yard	ya

SPORT

If you enjoy keeping fit and don't mind paying a fairly hefty fee, you could visit one of the health centres in the top hotels, such as the Grand Europe, the Astoria and Angleterre.

TOURIST INFORMATION

The main source of guidance for visitors to St Petersburg are not tourist information offices but the major hotels. Most of these provide a tour-booking service and the less central hotels have a Service Bureau.
Also useful is **Ost-West Kontaktservice**, tel: 327-3416, which runs a free tourist information service, sells books and maps and can book entertainment and accommodation for visitors.

Right: going home

FURTHER READING

Non-fiction

Russia, with Teheran, Port Arthur and Peking, Karl Baedeker, 1914. Re-issued by David & Charles, 1971. A classic travel guide to Imperial Russia.

Literary Russia: A Guide, Anna Benn and Rosamund Bartlett. Picador/Papermac, 1997.

'Guide to a Renamed City' in *Less than One*, Joseph Brodsky. Penguin, 1986.

St Petersburg: The Hidden Interiors, Katya Galitzine. Hazar, 1999.

Memoirs of a Blockade Survivor, Lidia Ginzburg. Harvill, 1997.

The Russian Experiment in Art, Camilla Gray. Thames & Hudson, 1962.

Peter the Great: His Life and Work, Robert K Massie. Abacus, 1981.

Pavlovsk: The Life of a Palace, Suzanne Massie. Hodder & Stoughton, 1990.

The Hermitage, Geraldine Norman. Pimlico, 1999.

St Petersburg: A Cultural History, Solomon Volkov. Simon & Schuster, 1995.

The Orthodox Church, Timothy Ware. Kallistos Ware, 1969.

The Amber Room: the Untold Story of the Greatest Hoax of the 20th Century, Adrian Levy, Catherine Scott-Clark. Atlantic Books, 2004. An intriguing investigation into the myth of Catherine Palace's legendary rooms.

Insight Guide: St Petersburg, Apa Publications *(various authors)*, 2004.

Insight Guide: Russia, Apa Publications *(various authors)*, 2004.

Compact Guide: Moscow, Leonid Bloch. Apa Publications, 2002.

Fiction

St Petersburg, Andrei Bely. Penguin, 1916.

Crime and Punishment, Fyodor Dostoevsky. Penguin, 2003. This new translation promises to make this most important work more accessible.

The Idiot, Fyodor Dostoevsky. Penguin 2004. A recent re-translation of this morality tale set in St Petersburg.

The Devils (The Possessed), Fyodor Dostoevesky. Penguin 1973. Perhaps his most political novel which confronts the spirit of revolution.

Diary of a Madman and Other Stories, Nikolai Gogol. Penguin, 1974. Includes 'The Nose', and other tales set in St Petersburg.

Glas: New Russian Writing, ed. Natasha Perova, UK subscriptions and enquiries (tel: 020-7414 6044).

Eugene Onegin, Alexander Pushkin. Penguin, 1831. A novel in verse.

Among the Russians, Colin Thubron. Heinemann/Penguin, 1983.

Anna Karenina, Leo Tolstoy. Penguin, 1876.

Poetry

The Twelve, Alexander Blok, Journeyman, (1918).

The Bronze Horseman, Alexander Pushkin, Secker (1859).

Selected Poems, Anna Akhmatava. Penguin 1992. The most gifted survivor of the seige of Leningrad.

practical information

St Petersburg Metro

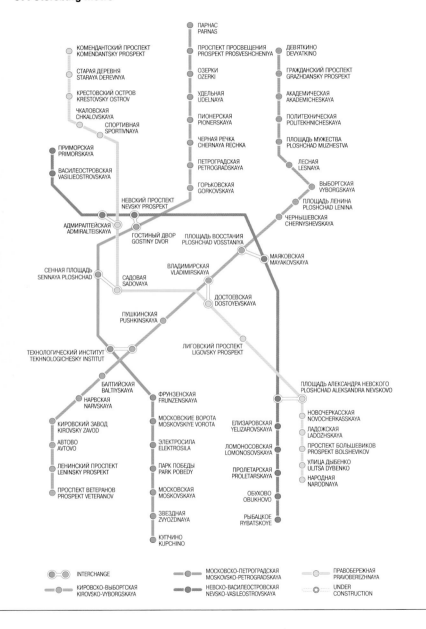

ПАРНАС
PARNAS

КОМЕНДАНТСКИЙ ПРОСПЕКТ
KOMENDANTSKY PROSPEKT

ПРОСПЕКТ ПРОСВЕЩЕНИЯ
PROSPEKT PROSVESHCHENIYA

ДЕВЯТКИНО
DEVYATKINO

СТАРАЯ ДЕРЕВНЯ
STARAYA DEREVNYA

ОЗЕРКИ
OZERKI

ГРАЖДАНСКИЙ ПРОСПЕКТ
GRAZHDANSKY PROSPEKT

КРЕСТОВСКИЙ ОСТРОВ
KRESTOVSKY OSTROV

УДЕЛЬНАЯ
UDELNAYA

АКАДЕМИЧЕСКАЯ
AKADEMICHESKAYA

ЧКАЛОВСКАЯ
CHKALOVSKAYA

ПИОНЕРСКАЯ
PIONERSKAYA

ПОЛИТЕХНИЧЕСКАЯ
POLITEKHNICHESKAYA

СПОРТИВНАЯ
SPORTIVNAYA

ЧЕРНАЯ РЕЧКА
CHERNAYA RECHKA

ПЛОЩАДЬ МУЖЕСТВА
PLOSHCHAD MUZHESTVA

ПРИМОРСКАЯ
PRIMORSKAYA

ПЕТРОГРАДСКАЯ
PETROGRADSKAYA

ЛЕСНАЯ
LESNAYA

ВАСИЛЕОСТРОВСКАЯ
VASILEOSTROVSKAYA

ГОРЬКОВСКАЯ
GORKOVSKAYA

ВЫБОРГСКАЯ
VYBORGSKAYA

НЕВСКИЙ ПРОСПЕКТ
NEVSKY PROSPEKT

ПЛОЩАДЬ ЛЕНИНА
PLOSHCHAD LENINA

АДМИРАЛТЕЙСКАЯ
ADMIRALTEISKAYA

ЧЕРНЫШЕВСКАЯ
CHERNYSHEVSKAYA

ГОСТИНЫЙ ДВОР
GOSTINY DVOR

ПЛОЩАДЬ ВОССТАНИЯ
PLOSHCHAD VOSSTANIYA

МАЯКОВСКАЯ
MAYAKOVSKAYA

СЕННАЯ ПЛОЩАДЬ
SENNAYA PLOSHCHAD

ВЛАДИМИРСКАЯ
VLADIMIRSKAYA

САДОВАЯ
SADOVAYA

ДОСТОЕВСКАЯ
DOSTOYEVSKAYA

ПУШКИНСКАЯ
PUSHKINSKAYA

ЛИГОВСКИЙ ПРОСПЕКТ
LIGOVSKY PROSPEKT

ТЕХНОЛОГИЧЕСКИЙ ИНСТИТУТ
TEKHNOLOGICHESKY INSTITUT

ПЛОЩАДЬ АЛЕКСАНДРА НЕВСКОГО
PLOSHCHAD ALEKSANDRA NEVSKOVO

БАЛТИЙСКАЯ
BALTIYSKAYA

ФРУНЗЕНСКАЯ
FRUNZENSKAYA

НОВОЧЕРКАССКАЯ
NOVOCHERKASSKAYA

НАРВСКАЯ
NARVSKAYA

МОСКОВСКИЕ ВОРОТА
MOSKOVSKIYE VOROTA

ЕЛИЗАРОВСКАЯ
YELIZAROVSKAYA

ЛАДОЖСКАЯ
LADOZHSKAYA

КИРОВСКИЙ ЗАВОД
KIROVSKY ZAVOD

ЭЛЕКТРОСИЛА
ELEKTROSILA

ЛОМОНОСОВСКАЯ
LOMONOSOVSKAYA

ПРОСПЕКТ БОЛЬШЕВИКОВ
PROSPEKT BOLSHEVIKOV

АВТОВО
AVTOVO

ПАРК ПОБЕДЫ
PARK POBEDY

ПРОЛЕТАРСКАЯ
PROLETARSKAYA

УЛИЦА ДЫБЕНКО
ULITSA DYBENKO

ЛЕНИНСКИЙ ПРОСПЕКТ
LENINSKY PROSPEKT

МОСКОВСКАЯ
MOSKOVSKAYA

НАРОДНАЯ
NARODNAYA

ПРОСПЕКТ ВЕТЕРАНОВ
PROSPEKT VETERANOV

ОБУХОВО
OBUKHOVO

ЗВЕЗДНАЯ
ZVYOZDNAYA

РЫБАЦКОЕ
RYBATSKOYE

КУПЧИНО
KUPCHINO

INTERCHANGE

МОСКОВСКО-ПЕТРОГРАДСКАЯ
MOSKOVSKO-PETROGRADSKAYA

ПРАВОБЕРЕЖНАЯ
PRAVOBEREZHNAYA

КИРОВСКО-ВЫБОРГСКАЯ
KIROVSKO-VYBORGSKAYA

НЕВСКО-ВАСИЛЕОСТРОВСКАЯ
NEVSKO-VASILEOSTROVSKAYA

UNDER
CONSTRUCTION

ACKNOWLEDGEMENTS

Photography except for	Anna Mockford *and* Nick Bonetti
31	akg-images London
10, 11	Bogdanovich
58B	Fritz Dressler
12, 13T/B, 14B, 15, 48	Grudenko
14T	Jurgens
Back cover left centre, 16, 21, 23, 32T/B, 34, 35B, 42, 45T, 47T, 49, 54, 59, 65, 69, 70, 72, 78, 79, 80, 86, 91	Tony Perrottet
2/3	Ed Pritchard/Stone/Getty Images
Cover	Wojtek Buss/Powerstock

Cartography	Berndtson & Berndtson
	Mike Larby

© APA Publications GmbH & Co. Verlag KG Singapore Branch, Singapore

credits

INDEX